MAXIMIZED

MAXIMIZED

v.t. (max" i' miz)
To attain or reach the highest
possible value or potential

Cathryn L. Taylor M.A. MFT LADC

iUniverse, Inc.
New York Lincoln Shanghai

MAXIMIZED
v.t. (max" i' miz)
To attain or reach the highest possible value or potential

iUniverse books may be ordered through booksellers or by contacting:

iUniverse
2021 Pine Lake Road, Suite 100
Lincoln, NE 68512
www.iuniverse.com
1-800-Authors (1-800-288-4677)

ISBN-13: 978-0-595-36279-0 (pbk)
ISBN-13: 978-0-595-80724-6 (ebk)
ISBN-10: 0-595-36279-6 (pbk)
ISBN-10: 0-595-80724-0 (ebk)

Printed in the United States of America

This book is dedicated to
Suzy and Allan Tabor
my sister and brother-in-law.

"...You have always been there assisting me in
"Maximizing"
my resources by being so gracious and generous
with your own..."

Contents

"The Initiation"

"...The drum starts its beat. The shamanic journey begins. I feel Max running at my heels. I wonder if he will be permitted to follow. I receive immediate confirmation that his presence is indeed divinely planned. Max and I are guided to another world. We are greeted by a host of power animals. Each gives us instructions on what our path is to be.

Master Wolf is the last to appear. He motions for us to sit before him. Wolf then retrieves a crystal and a sacred stone from Mother Earth. He ceremoniously implants the crystal into Max's third eye. The sacred stone is placed in the center of my heart. Its beat quickens—becomes synchronistic with the rhythm of the drum. The rhythm of the drum resonates with the pulse of Mother Earth.

There is attunement. There is silence. There is prayer.

Master Wolf speaks. "An initiation has just taken place. Max, you have been ordained a healer, and Cathryn, your heart, which suffers a wound of betrayal, has been touched and prepared for its healing..."

I was stunned. I had just experienced my first Shamanic journey, and I was absolutely stunned. Who was this wolf who had just appeared in my mind's eye? What did he mean I had a wounded heart? And Max, a healer? That thought alone intrigued me! But in no way was I prepared for the journey that was about to unfold—a journey whose affects would take me through dimensions of time and space which would forever change the way in which I viewed my world.

-----CHAPTER ONE-----

"The Beginning"

The other puppies rushed immediately to the front of their cages, yelping and jumping as if to say, "Pick me! Pick Me!" But not Max! Max sat with a regal air and nonchalant confidence, "I already know our destiny. You'll choose me." And I did—without a single hesitation—for I also knew, from the first moment I saw him, there would be a deep bond between us. There was just a spirit or essence within Max that commanded and deserved to be revered. In return, he offered a loyalty which quickly elevated his role from mere pet to one of teacher, companion, and best friend. Without him I would never have had the courage to heed the divine inspiration to sell everything I owned and embark on a road trip around the United States. Long before the encounter with Master Wolf, I was aware of how important Max had become in my life. In fact, when my so-called "divine plan" revealed itself, the one prayer I had made to God was to insure Max's safety.

The seeds of this "plan" came to light one morning when Max and I were taking our morning jog on the trails of Mount Tamalpais. Mount Tamalpais, or as the locals refer to her, Mt. Tam, is one of the most sacred places on earth. She rests in the center of Marin County—a county that serves as the northern anchor to the Golden Gate Bridge and has provided the stage upon which I have experienced my most profound spiritual encounters. On this particular day, as I jogged across the rolling belly of her earth, I paused long enough to listen. And as I did, the trees whispered in my ear, *"Let your heart relax and say good-bye to that which holds you captive."*

A chill ran down my spine.

I had been stuck for months. Often I prayed for direction, for some inspiration on what to do next, but I had never considered just "relaxing and letting go!" It's not my nature. The thought catapulted me into such a state of panic that I momentarily could not breathe.

Even though I was afraid of change, I was even more afraid that things would remain the same. I had been depressed for quite some time. It had started several years earlier when a long-term relationship had dissolved. It was not sudden. It was more like a long, slow death. I had suffered many losses in my life, but for some reason, when this relationship ended, something deep within me ceased to exist as well.

I had known for some time that relationships were my passion. I am a student of human behavior. This study is what gives my life meaning. It is the most profound expression of my spiritual gifts and my worldly ability to manifest relationships. The source of my passion had always been relating to others and then writing about what I experienced, felt and saw. I eagerly studied and recorded every interaction I encountered. It became my art and the world of relationships was the canvas upon which I created. I was as devoted to its practice as a concert pianist is to the piano. It was my life's work. Many yearn to experience intimacy. I had made it's pursuit a career. I made a career out of my passion to understand intimacy and used that understanding to help others more effectively relate.

This primary relationship had been my most significant source of study. When it ended, I lost my passion. I was perplexed, bewildered and depressed by this fact. I could not, for the life of me, comprehend why I felt so wounded by its dissolution.

The dissolution of a primary relationship may not have affected someone else in the same way. Others may have been able to move on, to find another venture in which they could invest. But for me, this relationship was the outgrowth of an inner passion that longed to experience and explore the intricacies of intimacy. My commitment involved a willingness to uncover anything within me that prohibited my ability to love with an open heart. When the possibility of that endeavor vanished, my relationship to my own passion changed as well. I no longer believed in it. My willingness to risk being vulnerable with another had always been a great source of self esteem. That very trait appeared to be the primary reason for the loss of my most valued relationship. I had been accused, for much of my life, of being "too intense." The ending of this vital relation-ship seemed to prove these accusations true. I began to believe it was the intensity of my passion that drove this man away. Confronting that possibility resulted in losing trust in my ability to relate. I doubted my capacity to make sound judgments with respect to anything in my life.

In addition, the recent release of my **_INNER CHILD WORKBOOK_** challenged me professionally in ways that demanded confidence and connectedness. The combination of these two events required more than I could be at that time. Tension led to depression and depression led to emotional collapse. Isolation became my norm. Though so unlike me...it felt as if I had little choice. My passion for taking risks simply dissolved; when it did, all trust vanished. I did not understand what was going on. I only knew I felt tremendous loss and despair. Unable to invest in a relationship with a person, I naturally turned to Max and the leash on him was becoming quite short. The other relationship that offered safety was the one I had with Mother Earth. Max and I spent hours hiking our favorite trails.

I had lost trust in my ability to relate and felt the need to avoid any situation that held potential for emotional involvement. Losing trust in one's self is a tragedy. Losing touch with one's passion—a true source of despair. I had become emotionally crippled and my world had become quite small. Within a short time, my focus was entirely on work. It was the one area in which I could continue the study of intimacy without risking personal hurt.

The core of my life's work centered on my being open and honest in my communications with myself and others and then teaching students and clients how to do the same. To witness myself avoiding the very passion that before had been the truest nourishment of my Soul was devastating. A year later, the situation had worsened. The part of me who was open, gregarious and eager to share was nowhere to be found. Without her I felt naked and shallow, empty with no vision, no purpose, and no passion for life.

I was depressed—and I knew I was depressed. Until that day on Mt. Tam, however, I had no antidote for my depression. I may have experienced panic when the message of the trees first reached my ears, but when the idea settled in, I felt relief. I didn't know what was about to unfold, but that unknowingness was refreshing compared to the dense, fog-like feeling of depression that had haunted me for so long.

Within days, an opportunity presented itself that could not be ignored. I received a call from a woman named Anna Maria. Anna Maria is a soft-spoken, yet intense and articulate Hispanic woman who goes after what she wants. There was a rapport from the first moment we talked. She had heard about my work and was intrigued enough to organize a group to participate in one of my Inner Child Workshops.

During these workshops I systematically guided participants through the seven developmental stages of childhood. Using my workbook as a guideline, the participants were given exercises which helped them identify the strengths and challenges of their past, learn new ways to cope and to become more successful, empowered adults. Anna Maria was not only the organizer of the class, she was also a participant. This avenue provided an arena in which our friendship grew. One morning, before class began, she pulled me to the side to tell me about a dream she had had recently in which she was scheduling workshops for me all over the country. She believed it was a dream inspired by the Divine...and expressed her interest in making the dream become a reality.

I, too, saw her dream as a message from the Divine and interpreted her offer as a personal nudge from God for me to take a risk. Her offer was the stimulus I needed to move from my self-constructed womb of depression to a world which held a destiny unknown.

Two weeks later I decided to sell everything I owned and began the necessary preparations to leave my home of fifteen years.

-----CHAPTER TWO-----

"Crossing the Bridge into the Unknown"

With workshops scheduled, belongings sold, and a motor home purchased, Max and I crossed that bridge into the unknown. The motivation had been despair, the inspiration, a gift from the divine. It was a radical change in lifestyle. The challenges seemed plentiful, the possibilities limitless.

There were limitations as well. Gone were the constants of a home address and phone number. Gone were the predictables of daily mail, client appointments and get-togethers with friends. Other than Max, every facet of my day-to-day life that offered a thread of familiarity and security had been traded in for an RV and the promise of adventure.

This pleased the nature of my Gemini Sun, but my Moon is in Cancer! Connection to a home base is vital. To appease this part of my personality, I had to find new ways to create a sense of connectedness. Well acquainted with the support available in the spiritual realm, I found myself in desperate need of stability in the physical one.

I had already come to rely on the comforts found in nature. Grandfather Sun was the friend with whom I most often shared my morning cup of tea; and it was Grandmother Moon who periodically peaked in my window to bid me farewell for the night. When I arrived at a new location for work, I searched immediately for a place where Max and I could run on the belly of Mother Earth and feel the spirits of the rocks and the trees. I didn't feel settled until this place had been found. I wanted to learn more about revering Mother Earth and to be around others who valued the same. I began the search for a community of like-minded people who would be accessible in most areas on my tour.

My travels to San Diego provided that opportunity. A Basic Shamanism workshop was being offered around the same time we had scheduled one of my classes. I knew very little about shamanism, but my American Indian heritage drew me naturally to these traditions first. Its community was widespread and it involved a practice that revered Mother Earth. I promptly registered. The workshop was amazing. We were taught the basic techniques of journeying. The first journey I did was the one in which Master Wolf officiated Max's and my initiation.

The next journey proved to be just as illuminating. We were instructed to go to the upper world and request a meeting with a teacher.

"...The clouds clear. I am met by an Indian Princess. She takes me to a clearing and instructs me to wait. Moments later an Indian Chief appears. In a voice that commands respect, he states, "I am here to help you deal with the areas of your life clouded by longings, attachments and fears."

Like Master Wolf, he, too, talks of betrayal. "It is time to confront this betrayal and learn how to feel safe in the physical as well as non-physical worlds. But first," he announces, "you must agree to a period of silence. It is a prerequisite to becoming my student—a test in discernment. Do you agree?"

A voice within me frantically begins to bargain..."Can I at least share my experiences with one or two friends," she pleas. It is the Gemini within me, the part who thrives on talking and telling stories.

With arms folded, Chief looks away, unamused. I wince and say to myself, "This is going to be more serious than I had thought...not much room for humor in this exchange!" I fidget a bit and then reluctantly agree. Chief gestures that the meeting is over and motions for the Indian Princess to assist me on my return to "ordinary time."

On the journey back she turns to me and inquires, "Did you recognize him?"

I think for a moment and then reply, "Well, yes, he did look familiar."

"He was the guardian angel of your father. They still work together today. It was his hand that your father took when he left this world and crossed over to the

other side. You saw him then. You saw him take your
father's hand the moment you let it go..."
  I REMEMBERED AND I CRIED.

Being present at the moment of my father's death
had been one of the richest moments in my life. I sat
with him for his last five days. We talked and cried and
I shared with him what he could expect when the time
came for him to leave. The moment Dad took his last
breath, I saw the essence of, what I believed to be, his
guardian angel. He was an Indian Chief of great
stature. The same Indian Chief appeared in my meditation three days later to tell me that he had successfully escorted my father to the other side. Dad had
made his transition with ease. I had not seen the
Indian Chief since. And now, five years later, he was
appearing in my inner work, speaking to me about
safety and betrayal. I had no more clue as to what he
referred, than when Master Wolf spoke of betrayal. I
did have the sense that Dad's Guardian Angel had some
very important Teachings for me.

Over the next three weeks, Chief and I met often in
my daily meditations. He gave me Teachings about how
to walk in harmony with Mother Earth, how to notice
and revere all living things. I looked forward to our
encounters. It was like meeting with a wise old friend.

As my work in San Diego came to a close, the intensity of my work with Chief lessened as well. The work
had been great, the meditations revealing, but I
needed a break. My next workshop was scheduled in
San Francisco in two weeks. I headed back up north.

The trip up the California coast was relaxing and reflective. I thought a great deal about my experiences with the teachings from Chief. I pondered what they all meant and began to suspect that Chief had perhaps come into my meditations now to assist me in yet another layer of betrayal, loss and grief. It was not long before my suspicions were confirmed.

-----CHAPTER THREE-----

"Getting the Bad News"

I wanted a week of vacation, but God gave me five days. I had noticed blood in Max's urine so I took him to the Vet. It did not look good. We were referred to a specialist for some tests.

   "...We walk into the reception room. The walls are lined with cold, red bricks. The floor is covered with stark, black tiles intended to resist the stains of incontinent and nauseous pets dragged reluctantly through these doors. The nurse escorts us to a room in the back. We sit. We wait. Twenty minutes later the radiologist runs breathlessly into the room. He profusely apologizes for the wait. I am too nervous to accept his apology. I want him to look at my dog, to give him the necessary medicine and go home.
   It doesn't turn out that way. There are additional tests he has to run. They require sedation. Max will have to stay. He promises to call me as soon as the tests are complete. He leaves as abruptly as he had entered.

His assistant enters the room and clips a generic leash onto Max's collar. I give him a quick kiss good-bye and she briskly leads him away.

Anxiety pulsates through my veins. I go to the mountain to try to outrun my fears. I am too restless to succeed. I return home and try to chase away the fears by busying myself with errands. It doesn't work. Nothing affects the fear until I hear the ringing of the phone. The fear is then replaced by sheer terror. The tests are complete, but the nurse will say no more except that Max is ready to come home. I drive back to the clinic.

This time, when I enter its doors, I am met by the Vet himself. He greets me and requests that I follow him. I do as I am told. On the way to the examination room he pauses, clears his throat, turns to me and says, "You have a very sick dog..."

His "diagnostic" words dangled in the air—threatening to sever the last thread of safety I had in this world. I burst into tears. A colleague walked up to him and began to discuss a procedure she had just completed. Their exchange distracted him from the task at hand. I am left, unattended. Moments, that seemed like hours, passed. With little grace, I unexpectedly spurt out, "Excuse me, could we get on with this!!" Alarmed by my outburst, he embarrassedly turned around. I got the impression that he had forgotten I was even there.

I came close to losing control. I wanted to scream, "Just tell me what's wrong with my dog!!!" But I kept my cool. We walked to the examination room where an assistant was waiting with Max. Although drowsy, he pulled from her grasp, leaped up and planted two paws in the center of my chest. It was his way of saying hello. My eyes filled with tears. I told myself the Vet must be wrong. He showed me the x-rays. He wasn't...

He described the situation, but I did not hear a word. All I could see was the dark spot on the screen. I had seen this image before. I knew it is not good.

Then the Vet says words that I do hear.

"...Your dog has a cancerous tumor on his bladder. I don't know how he has made it this long. At most, he has two to three weeks to live."

...I am speechless. Without saying thank you or good-bye, I lead Max out of the room, pay the bill and walk out of the clinic in a daze.

It's raining. Max and I make it to the car. There is little distinction between my tears and the raindrops falling on the windshield. Max finds his way to my lap. We just sit there. I cannot move. I hold onto Max wondering how I am ever going to let him go..."

In the emptiness of the moment I remembered a card a friend had given me of a Spiritual healer. I frantically retrieved it from my purse, grabbed the car phone and dialed. The phone rang and then I heard, "Hello."

"...I begin telling my story only to soon realize that the voice on the other end of the line is recorded. I pause and catch my breath while the message plays

out. I have never met this man, yet, just the sound of his voice steadies the palpitations of my heart. Words, muffled by my sobs, convey our need for help. The rawness of my plea leaves me feeling extremely vulnerable, but it is not a time to be shy. We need help and this man is the first to whom we turn. Once the call is made, I find the courage and the fortitude to drive home. It is one of the longest trips of my life..."

I have no idea how I made it through that first night. It was horrible. I was in shock. I was to start a full month Inner Child Workshop the next day with a group of participants I had never before seen. I had no idea how I was ever going to manage. All I could to do was cry. I wasn't ready to lose my best friend. He was the only being in the world for whom I felt complete trust. I was not ready to live my life without him.

The Spiritual Healer finally responded to my call. Greg is a practitioner who was trained in China and does hands-on spiritual healing. He explained that he primarily worked with humans, but he had also worked with animals. His next opening was in a week. I hysterically proclaimed that we didn't have that kind of time. He suggested I bring him a picture of Max and offered to do some "healing in abstentia" work over the weekend. I wasn't sure what Greg meant, but he was recommended by a highly-trusted friend, and at that time, there were few left in that category. I took him the picture of Max.

I tried to turn my focus back to my work. It wasn't easy. I could not fathom how I was ever going to conduct a workshop, knowing that Max could expire at any minute. I struggled with the little decisions. Should I take him with me, as I always did, or should I leave him home? If I left him home I would constantly worry if he were all right. If I brought him with me, I feared it may provoke so much grief that I would not be able to cope and teach.

It dawned on me how much of an integral part of my work Max had truly become. He was in every class, every consultation—by my side practically every minute of my day. Comprehending the totality of the inevitable loss was overwhelming. What made it even more difficult was that distancing from the pain and getting lost in my work did not seem like an option.

Most professions offer an escape from one's personal life. A lawyer or a proctologist can go to work and forget, at least for awhile, the traumas of every day life. But to work in the manner in which I am accustomed, I had to have emotional, physical, as well as, spiritual clarity. Besides being the only source of intimacy that still remained, maintaining a connection to my higher source and staying open to my feelings is the very core of who I am as a therapist and teacher. It is one of the occupational hazards of my field and, at that time, it was a challenge. I relied heavily on my support from the spiritual realm; it was my only choice. The grief was too big and the fear too consuming.

The next morning I began the new Workshop. Max was by my side. He had no visible signs of being sick. He simply did as he always did—slept under the desk and dreamt his doggie dreams.

The first day was manageable. I had been given a reprieve from the grief while I bonded and began with this new class.

The second day, however, was not.

"...I awake to a tear-drenched pillow. I don't want to get out of bed. I force myself to sit up. As I do so I involuntarily begin to rock myself back and forth, as if I am a small child, seeking comfort from some unknown source.

Then, almost as if guided by an invisible force, I am out of bed dressing in the outfit I had worn when I gave a keynote address at a conference coordinated by a friend who worked at the Betty Ford Center. The talk had been one of my most successful professional moments. Wearing these clothes seems to give me a way to access the "self" who will be able to conduct the workshop. She is the only competent and reliable me who has the professional strength to carry on.

I am definitely over-dressed for the occasion. It is the day I facilitate the regression to infancy. The participants tease me about my being all dressed up on the day they have to crawl around on the floor sucking on baby bottles! I can see their point. I laugh with them, but offer no explanation. It is too soon to make this crisis public..."

There were many moments during this time when my behavior appeared a bit odd. But I had to respond to the parts within me who were in pain. Max was too important to me. Even if no one else could understand the depth of my pain, I had to honor it.

I also held onto the belief that there was a higher purpose to this situation, and a hope that if I could "just figure it out," Max may not have to leave.

I absolutely could not accept that I might lose him. The panic was too great. I had to hold onto the hope for a cure. It was the only source of courage that enabled me to proceed.

Max responded positively to the sessions with Greg. I noticed a difference in the amount of blood in his urine right away. I also took him to Lisa, a Shaman I had met through the workshop in San Diego. When she saw Max come bouncing into her living room, she said, "This is not a dog who has decided to die." Her words were music to my ears.

She did a journey. When she came back she reported that Max's power animals had come forth to assist her. There were seven Wild Dogs, and they each offered a piece of healing. The Chief of Dogs instructed her to tell me that I should journey for Max each day and call them in for assistance.

I was more than willing to do this. I reflected on the initiation—but now with a different eye. I still could not help but wonder how Max's illness was going to affect the healing of my heart. Was my healing, in fact, to be a result of my healing him? Was this perhaps the true purpose of the shamanic training—to have the techniques I would need to assist in Max's healing?

It wasn't long before my questions were answered. In the first journey I conducted for Max, Chief appeared. He confirmed that part of my training had been to prepare me to work with Max. He further explained that Max would respond most positively to the medicines administered to him from his own world—the animal world. In order to access those medicines, I had to be willing to go to that world. The shamanic journey provided an avenue to accomplish that task.

I began journeying. Chief was always by my side. The results were amazing. The Wild Dogs continued to be the main source of healing. They did power dances around Max, systematically entering his system to dissolve the infliction.

"...One day, after finishing his work with Max, Chief Dog came up to me and authoritatively said, "Give him some red meat, get him back to nature and take that darn leash off him. Free him so he can find the strength within to heal..."

It was somewhat disconcerting. Being reprimanded by a wild dog that appears in one's inner eye is a bit strange. But, I dutifully got Max some chunks of organic red meat and took him to Mt. Tam without a leash.

Another time the Wild Dogs came and, with great calculation, used their fire breath, to burn out the tumor. When it was burnt to a crisp, with one fell swoop, one of the Chief Dogs bit the tumor off in his mouth and abruptly turned to spit it into my hand. I was then instructed to take what I was seeing in my mind's eye and to physicalize it by drawing a picture of the tumor on paper with pen. I was to then burn the paper and take the ashes up to Mother Earth with an offering of gratitude for the healing that was taking place. I drew the picture and went immediately to the mountain.

There was a message from the radiologist when I returned. He had talked with a specialist in Berkeley. She thought she could help. An appointment had been scheduled for the end of that week.

She assessed that Max would respond to one or two chemotherapy treatments. At first I felt reticent to subject him to such a procedure. As she explained it, however, I began to understand it was not the same as it is for humans. Although he would feel a little sick, he would not lose his hair, and his discomfort would last only a few days. In exchange, the chemotherapy would shrink the tumor enough so that the bleeding would diminish and his flow would improve. It could extend his life for perhaps six months to a year.

I came back and called Greg. I needed to talk it over with someone. I was concerned about doing too many kinds of treatments. To my surprise, Greg explained that it could actually enhance his work with Max. A few chemo therapy treatments could potentially stop, even reduce, the growth, giving us the time we needed to possibly turn the situation around.

I took all of this information in, but still felt queasy about the whole idea. Did I have a "right" to intervene in the natural course of this crisis? I questioned whether I would be doing it for Max's comfort or my need to delay the inevitable grief.

That night I went over to Joy's house. She has been a colleague and friend for more than a decade. We often exchanged our respective skills. Joy carries the persona of a "Heloise." She can always come up with at least a few "hints" of resolution for even the most out-rageous situations. One of her skills is that of being trained in using a dowser. The dowser is an instrument which measures the electromagnetic field of an object and responds with a yes or no answer to questions that are addressed either to the subject or to the Higher Power of that subject. The art is in knowing how to phrase the questions so that they can be answered with a simple yes or no reply. The key in using some-thing such as this is to never rely solely on it for a decision. One does not give power away to a metal object,—at least I don't.

"...We begin our inquiries with Max. The minute we direct our attention to him, he starts "talking to us" by moaning and wagging his tail. It is quite dear.

We ask if he is ready to die. The dowser reads his answer as yes.

We ask if he is in pain. The wire fluctuates between yes and no. We ask if he likes his work with Greg. The dowser swings an emphatic yes!

We ask if he is receptive to the chemotherapy treatment. At first the reply is No. We ask if he is afraid. It indicates that this is the case. I take a few moments to explain the procedure. I speak to him as I would a human friend. He seems to comprehend because when asked again, the dowser indicates that he agrees..."

Finally, Max had had enough. He came over and nudged me on the leg. It was his signal that he wanted to go outside. After a short walk we began to use the dowser on me.

Once attuned to my Higher Self, we used a series of questions to deduct that my task was to heal the adult self who did not want to let go of Max because she did not want to travel alone. She did not want to travel alone because she felt unsafe. Her lack of safety was related to her wounded heart.

I recalled the Initiation by Master Wolf. I could not understand how losing Max would facilitate the healing of my heart. It seemed, instead, as though it were breaking it in two.

Trying to imagine life without Max was unbearable, almost impossible. He was such an intricate part of every moment of my day. And yet, deep within me, I felt a willingness to confront and process the inner pain. I would not turn my back on Max or turn away from the feelings of grief which I knew would accompany my staying emotionally present until the end. Although not always appreciative of this fact, the inevitable loss of him had indeed re-awakened the sleeping passion within me. My healing had begun.

-----CHAPTER FOUR-----

"Chasing the Cat Energy Away"

I decided to go through with several chemotherapy treatments to see how Max would respond. On the morning of his first treatment I awoke early to do a journey.

"...Chief greets me then leads me to the Wild Dogs. They are holding camp near Max's physical form. Tiger appears. Her first healing is on me. She wraps me up, mummy style, in a healing, violet light. She twirls me around counter-clockwise to align my energy, then leads me to Max's power animals. They instruct me to purchase a small portion of red meat and to then take Max to the mountain so a preparatory ritual can be performed..."

When we arrive, I find our place of meditation and again close my eyes.

"...A pack of Wild Dogs enters Max's body through an opening in the area of his solar plexus. They position themselves so they can run the "poison" to the tumor

without affecting the rest of his system. I am told to feed him two bites of red meat. It will give him the energy to withstand the procedure.

I envision the room in which he will be treated. I fill it with light and ask that the angels attend and stand watch. Chief assures me he will oversee the procedure as well. He summons a band of Indian Warriors and directs them to encircle the room and to protect its energy during the ordeal. I say a prayer asking that the Vet and the assisting technicians be guided by the Divine.

When the journey is complete, a Wild Dog comes up and licks my cheek. At the same moment I am seeing this in my mind's eye, Max comes up and does the same to my hand. The synchronicity anchors that which exists in the unseen into that being viewed by the human eye. The mission is complete..."

I drove Max to Berkeley, and then went to Mt. Tam to spend my day in prayer and meditation. I wrote affirmations, worked with the healing energy of the angels and stayed very connected to my Source.

More and more I found myself using the metaphysical principles to set the intention in the unseen and the shamanic practices to anchor those intentions into the earth plane. I felt blessed to be somewhat educated in both schools of thought; each seemed to enhance the other.

I picked Max up at the designated time. He was drowsy and withdrawn. Concerned and full of guilt and doubt about my decision, I tried to nurture and pet him, but he did not respond. I was looking for reassurance that he was in agreement with this course; but he was too ill to respond to my needs. He just wanted to be left alone. I respected his need for solitude and retired for yet another sleepless night.

The next morning I was startled awake by the sensation of a cat jumping on my face. It meant no harm. It had come to take Max away. I was still in a detached, semi-conscious state.

"...The cat's presence barely affects me. I calmly ask how long I have before Max must leave. It replies. "Not immediately, maybe a week or two."

Something doesn't feel right. I become conscious enough to recall my fear of cats. Why do I not feel fear now? I instinctively ask my Guidance if the cat is from the light or the dark.

There is no answer. Intuitively, I yell out, "In the name of the Light, I demand an answer!"

The cat vanishes. The sound of my own voice awakens the parts of me who still sleep. I sit up in bed alarmed..."

As I pondered this incident over a cup of morning tea, it seemed evident that the cat symbolized my fear of losing Max. I was being attacked by this fear but, in this semi-conscious state, I recognized the fear was not of the Light. I realized, at this very deep, inner level, I was not threatened by my own fear, at least at the moment when the cat made its visit. I had, therefore been able to see the cat for what it clearly was, and instinctively did what needed to be done to eradicate it. I had confronted the manifestation of my own vulnerability and, for the time being, the threat of the "cat energy" was gone.

Max's reactions to the treatment, however, were not. He was despondent for days. It unnerved me. Eventually, his appetite returned and after a session with Greg there was a noticeable difference. A few days later his urine was clear of blood and his flow had greatly improved.

When Max felt better we went up to Mt. Tam. While there, I meditated and asked for divine guidance on how best to proceed. I was told that if I were to be shown the lessons that were before me I would have to agree to begin to work on dissolving the symbiotic tie that existed between Max and me—that meant literally as well as symbolically. It meant taking the leash off and, unless there was a danger to him or others, giving him the freedom he deserved and needed in order to heal. I agreed, but not without a great deal of grief. The task of "letting go and letting God" is not as easy as it sounds!

I continued to do the journeys for Max. One day Chief instructed me to place my hands directly on Max's body. I followed Chief's instructions and immediately felt the healing energy flow through me. I could especially feel the warmth and heat coming through my right hand. As I did this, Max began to move his body closer into mine. Chief then directed me to lift my hands up and to reach out to the universe. The journey began.

"*...A White Snake appears. Chief explains that it is requesting to be blown into Max. It is a medicine Snake. It slithers into Max's body and begins to clean his urinary path. As the healing takes place, Chief counsels me. He advises me that I have to deal with my dependency upon Max and confront the fact that the outcome is not within my control. He reminds me of the crystal in Max's third eye and the stone that had been placed in the center of my heart. By activating and visualizing both of these, energy can radiate between us and a healing can occur in whatever form it is to take.*

White Raven comes forward. I know from my work with the Medicine Cards that Raven is the bringer of magic. If Raven appears in your vision, you are about to experience a change in consciousness. The thought fills me with anticipation. It seems significant and feels comforting that the raven is white—the color of healing. The White Raven flies around Max three times and then comes to me and says, "You want magic? I will give you magic." I blow him into Max's crown chakra.

He performs his magic. He dissolves the blood clots on the sides of the walls of the bladder and then breathes a soothing liquid through the passage in Max's belly. His beak pierces the tumor. White Raven fills up with the poison and flies away. I stand witness as he releases the poison into Mother Earth. She absorbs and dissolves it with her golden intention filled with love..."

The journey comes to an end. Its affects stay with me for a long time. But not forever. Shortly after this experience, I collapsed into the very fear I had just so gallantly challenged when visited by the energy of the cat.

I was afraid to be attached to Max's getting better because I was afraid that my level of need might sabotage the healing. I feared falling apart if he did die. I didn't want to project my needs on to him. I didn't want to admit that I did care if he died. I was trying to be more "spiritual" than all of me was, thus ignoring the voices inside who were in absolute panic. Some parts within had simply not attained that level of Divine nonchalance.

Learning to balance my soul's task to remain detached with my personality's need to hold on was definitely one of the higher lessons of this ordeal. Attaining that balance would be a definite challenge. There was a very strong part of me who just did not want to lose Max. I wanted him to stay. One day, in total desperation, I brought him to my lap and heard myself beg, "Please Max, stay with me, at least until the tour is over, so I can return home to heal. I don't think I can bear to lose you on the road. Can we agree to orchestrate your healing so we can at least complete this journey together as it began?"

Max looked at me and tilted his head as though to say, "Whatever you need, I'll do my best to succeed."

The journeys continued to be overseen by Chief and orchestrated by White Raven. White Raven was a special spiritual guide. In one journey he went to the underworld and returned with a beautiful pink crane. Crane enveloped Max's belly with her pink radiance and created a body blanket of protection over him. She then invited me to place my hands under the body blanket and to open myself up so my love for Max could be used as a conduit for the universal healing. When I did this, I felt the light begin to flood through my crown chakra.

On another journey White Raven took Max and I on his back to this sacred place in the universe where there was a beautiful column of light. The rest of the scene was pitch black.

"...I am instructed to sit in the middle of the light and use my love as a conduit to channel healing energy into the belly of Max's body. Inquiring as to why our surroundings are so black, Chief explains that we are in the center of a very sacred place, a place where all things are possible. American Indian tradition holds the belief that the color black is indeed sacred. Black holds every possibility in the universe. All medicines are available in the richness of its hue. Chief further explains that Max and I need to sit where there are no limitations on what can occur.

As I sit with my hands on Max's body, Hawk flies in to sit for a spell. Owl follows, and Bear, a bunch of Butterflies, the White Snakes, an Antelope, a Tiger...then White Raven reappears and asks to be blown into Max's physical form. I still have no idea how Raven fits into the bigger picture, but this time he opens up the passage ways and chews away the tumor.

Raven then ascends into the light and takes the tumor to the Grand Central Sun where it is pulverized. The tumor breaks into magnificent tiny particles of beauty.

I am so overcome by this image that tears begin to roll down my cheeks. I suddenly see the beauty and higher purpose of this cancerous growth. Once its true purpose is revealed, its dust is spread over Max's body to effectuate and contribute to the healing of his physical form.

Max's spirit then elevates above his body. I ask it if it wants to reside in Max anymore. There is a strong affirmative yes, but in the background I hear a whisper, "no."

I ask the part of Max who said "no" to step forward. It is a smaller version of Max. This little pup carries the toxins of the growth. As soon as he emerges, the bigger part of Max steps forward and starts licking the sick inner part, assuring him it will be all right. Max tells his "inner puppy" that he will gladly heal him and nurse him back to health. I stand in awe of this exchange. It is the first time I feel gratitude and can see what this tumor is in actuality offering..."

That wounded pup was a vital part of Max. It had absorbed multiple emotions from my clients as well as me. The experience was indeed giving both Max and I an opportunity to step into the ascended healers within us. It felt good to see it as a blessing and not a curse.

Though touched, I could not help but crack a smile. How many would get to witness a session of inner puppy work with their canine friend other than someone who had made her living doing the same with herself and others. I concluded that we do indeed "create our own reality!!!" Inner Puppy work! Even today it makes me smile and remember Max with such fondness!

The Workshop was over and I was getting ready to once again go on the road. This time it was up to the northwest. I had a very tight feeling in my stomach; I was afraid to leave. I was afraid to be away from my support system in the bay area. I did not know how I would cope if Max got really sick in a strange place. I wouldn't have Greg, my own Vet or any of my friends who had supported me during that first month. And I hated leaving without knowing if Max would be with me when I returned.

Most of all, I was afraid the cat energy would return. As our departure neared, it seemed ever-present, lurking in the shadows, preying on my mind and my soul. Who was this cat? What part of me carried such fear? Did I have the internal structure needed to keep chasing this cat energy away? Would I know how to discern the need to let go, to take charge or to just let it be? Those were the challenges that were around the bend—and they were challenges I was reluctant to meet.

-----CHAPTER FIVE-----

"On the Road Again"

With Max riding shot gun we headed up North. This time the destination was Montana. The drive through Nevada was comforting. I welcomed the vastness and openness of the desert. The lack of stimuli was a relief. I liked these drives from one city to the next. They gave me the proper time to digest the last experience as I readied myself for the next.

This drive was proving to me just how difficult the last month had truly been. Although prosperous emotionally and spiritually, it had taken its physical toll. Max, too, showed signs of wear. Still recuperating from his second chemotherapy treatment, he was docile for most of the trip. Finally, he began to bounce back. My car, however, did not. When I arrived, I realized I had towed it all the way up to Montana without taking it out of gear. The transmission was shot.

The metaphor of this incident was spellbinding. My car, my vehicle of transformation, had been stripped of its power, stripped because of my neglect.

Embracing this truth shattered something within me that was so vital, primal and core that I lost the internal balance that had been holding the veil of fear and regret intact. The way I had neglected my car became a mirror for how I had neglected Max, which became a mirror for how I was now neglecting myself. I had been hanging on to the illusion that I was handling this crisis quite well. Evidently that was not the case. I tumbled down a stairway of shame and guilt and landed in a dungeon of self-recrimination and blame. The voices that greeted me were vile. Their accusations: cold, wet and without mercy.

   "...It is you who caused this cancer. All of those times you fed him scraps instead of healthy food! Max has handled your stress and distress and emotional bouts and now look at his reward! It should be your tumor, not his! Because of your neglect and greed, he must now die! How could you be so selfish, so stupid and unaware? And now, look, not only do you trash you own life and Max's as well, you can't even show respect to the vehicle that has so faithfully transported you from place to place. You should be ashamed of yourself. You should suffer the pain—not him!"

   Compassion and forgiveness are nowhere in sight. I huddle in the corner of my shame and doubt. In response to some unknown prompting, I look up. I can hardly believe what I see. Reaching to me are the hands of Angels. When our hands touch, I feel an instant sense of peace and love.

One speaks, *"We are here to tell you that it is now safe to let Max go. It is not that he has to die, that decision has not been made. But your need for him to be sick has dissolved. You need to bring your meditations back to you. Max has been faithfully doing for you what you were unable—and unwilling—to do for yourself. But you now need to take responsibility for keeping your own physical, emotional and mental bodies clear. It will free Max to heal. You must now give Max's body permission to deal with his tumor. Bring in the power animals from his world to do the work. His spirit has never been more alive and more ready to be present. Tell Max he no longer has to meet your needs. He senses you are able to now take care of yourself. You need to come to know the same! It is time to put into practice what he has taught and you have learned..."*

The meditation continued and I was tapped on the shoulder by White Raven. He had a gold ribbon in his beak. He asked to be blown into Max's crown chakra. He flew regally to the tumor and gracefully tied a ribbon around it. The tumor slowly released itself and fell into a basket woven of the hair of the Angels and the feathers of Master Eagle. White Raven then flew to Great Mystery and made an offering to the Great Central Sun.

A turquoise Snake requested entry, along with seven Wild Dogs. Snake did a healing dance in the area that carried the pain. The area turned to the most beautiful color of healthy pink I had ever seen.

The seven wild dogs howled and danced and paid their respects. When the healing was done, the tumor had been removed.

I was told there would be some blood on the physical, but that this healing had freed Max to decide if he wanted to stay or go. The healing continued, but this time the focus was on me.

I am enveloped in a cloud of the unknown. I feel a sense of apprehension as I wait to see what will next appear. It is Chief. He requests that I take the stone that he holds in the palm of his hand and place it near my heart. I hold the stone to my chest and ask for clarity on what I am to do next.

All of a sudden the Indian Princess reappears. She is dressed in buckskin attire and is as radiant and beautiful as ever. She tells me she will now travel with me. I ask who she is. She says,

"...I am a part of you. I am who you will soon be. But before you can walk my path you have to face the fears Max has so dutifully carried for you. As you let go of your need for him to do this, you will gain the strength and ability to cope with these inner fears yourself. As you do...you will naturally become me."

Bewildered, I ask, "Can I call on you, and if so, what is your name?" She replies, "It is not time for such an exchange. Your new name will be given to you at a later time. I am the essence of your future self. You are not yet ready to become me—you still wear the cloak of your vulnerabilities and the issue with Max has scraped them to their very core. In the midst of this core is

*your work. Follow the you who exists in that role and
you will find your way to me..."*

Promise resonated in what she said. There was a
fresh authenticity that was beginning to emerge in my
encounters with others. The more vulnerable I became
in my personal life, the more depth I brought into my
consultations with others. Although sometimes difficult, the exposure allowed a genuineness to come
forth. When I was real, those with whom I worked felt
permission to be real as well. The line that needed to
be respected was the line that dictated the difference
between a consultation and the times I was around
them when I was not being paid for my time. Students
or participants of one of these workshops paid me to
teach them the skills needed to resolve their issues.
During those allotted hours, my attention was theirs. I
disclosed only that which might be helpful in their
work. But in traveling around in this way, there were
times when we were around each other and I was not
being paid for my time. It was then that I felt more
freedom to be real with my own vulnerability. This
duality enabled me to make more authentic connections
with those to whom I taught. The line was always challenging however, and being on the road challenged it
even more. In fact, everything about this journey was
challenging.

The process of letting go of Max had been continu-
ous since his diagnosis. As I released him, I stepped
more and more into the "protector and provider" part
of me. This relationship epitomized my attachments.
Resolving my dependency on Max allowed me to become

more autonomous and available to others. Nonetheless, it was difficult.

After my work in Montana was finished I returned, for a brief period, to the Bay Area. It felt wonderful to be around those with whom I felt so much support. Still, they were difficult months. I continued with the healings, but after the third chemotherapy treatment, Max just did not bounce back. There were moments when I thought things were turning around, but then there were just as many moments when I felt despair and lack of hope.

Finally, I was ready to begin the last scheduled leg of the tour. I had one month to get to Minnesota. Mom was going on the road trip with me. We were traveling the southern route so we could visit Sedona, Arizona. The day before I left, my Godchild and her father came over.

Lily was five years old. She had known Max all of her life. She had used him as her pillow when she had lounged around the house. He had humored her as she, with leash in hand, led him back and forth across he kitchen floor. He had chased balls and objects. She had thrown him tidbits of unwanted food. They were buddies, and now they somehow had to say what may well be their very last good-byes. It was a heartfelt afternoon. We took pictures of Lily, Max and me...and then went to the mountain for a walk. When our walk was almost over I turned around to take one last look. Max was running around the bend...I swallowed deeply, sensing it would be the last time he would share this walk with me in the flesh. The agony of that thought rested in my stomach like a bout of the emotional flu. I could not envision coming up to our sacred place without Max running close behind.

-----CHAPTER SIX-----

"The Circles of Healing"

That first week back on the road was hell. By the time Mom and I arrived in Flagstaff, Max's bleeding had increased. I was up with him until dawn. He was leaking blood all over. To protect the bed I had to go buy the bed protectors a mother would use for a new born infant. I called an emergency Veterinarian hospital, but they could do nothing until the next morning. When we did go, the Vet could only give me more pills and tell me it did not look good. I was afraid when I arrived at my mother's home in Nebraska I would have to put Max to sleep before I left for Minneapolis.

I was at odds with that possibility. Was it time to intervene? I could not imagine doing a workshop without Max. I could not imagine continuing the journey without him.

Several days into the trip we were driving toward Santa Fe. Mom was sleeping and Max was resting on my lap. I was totally exhausted. I had not slept all night. Max had not improved. He was now wearing diapers whenever he was indoors. I feared he would expire at any second. In the silence of the moment, I started to pray and cried out:

"...I don't know what to do! Please help me, God; I just don't know what to do!"

In my mind's eye, Jesus appears. He takes me by the hand and leads me to the sacred place in the sky. In the middle of the darkness he invites me to sit in a column of light. He places Max between us. Jesus then tells me to call a Healing Circle. I am not sure what he means. He instructs me to just mentally put out the word that I need help and assures me "they" will come. I feel like Kevin Costner in <u>Field of Dreams</u>, but I am not about to argue with Jesus!!! I welcome the Divine support.

The first one to arrive is Mother Mary. She comes and sits by my side. Then Greg comes. My friends, Sue, and Joy, Darlene, Marsha, Margee, and Anna Maria join the circle as well. Jesus then sits next to Max and begins to give him a transfusion of light. I hold the image for a long while. Mom suddenly awakes. I am startled back to every day time..."

Three hours later, I heard a knock in the center of my mind. It was not a sound that could be heard by anyone else in the world, but it was one that was as real to me as my breath. On the other side of the knock was my friend, Alyssa. She had just gotten the message. I received another message from Candace. She had gotten the call but could not show up right away because she was too burdened by work. The day went on like this. Different people kept showing up in my head. I even received an imaginary card from my first publisher, wishing us well. These visions were spontaneous, not self-induced. I did not try to imagine these responses. The images freely presented themselves to me in my mind's eye. It was quite wonderful and real.

By the time we arrived in Nebraska the bleeding had diminished and Max had improved. Unfortunately, I hadn't. My condition had worsened. Although inspired by the calling of the Healing Circle, I was worn down. Irritable and impatient, I was difficult to be around.

It was beyond me to stay unattached. I was happy when I sensed that Max had decided to stay and I could ready myself to grieve if his decision was to leave. What I could not do was reside in the middle of the unknown. Having no clue as to what would transpire was more than I could withstand. Like a needy buzzard, I hovered over Max, depriving him of his own decision. I tried to control, to fix, to do something, because doing nothing left me in too much pain.

I needed to pull my focus back to me, but I didn't seem to have the will. The part of me who was so afraid, who could not just relax and let things unfold, disgusted and angered me.

I tried to comfort myself and assure myself that the transition did not have to be so dramatic. I tried to keep in mind that whether Max lived six days, six weeks or six months, my task was to meet the daily challenges his illness brought to my front door. I tried to accept the fact that I did not have control over this situation. I was not particularly successful. I failed to understand how I was to proceed with the meditations and the attempts to heal without feeding the illusion that Max's destiny was in my hands.

How could I hold the intention for health and at the same time maintain the respect Max deserved for doing whatever he felt and chose to do? How could I take action without having an investment in its outcome? Those were the questions with which I wrestled. Retaining hope was a battle I had to constantly fight, and ultimately, it was a battle that I lost.

My hope vanished. I collapsed into anguish and self-doubt. I felt betrayed by my belief in everything I had done. I was fed up with shamanism, spiritual healing, vitamins, meditations and faith that this could be turned around. Max was not getting better, and I hated it. My hate turned to anger, then to apathy and despair.

One afternoon, while taking a drive along the country roads of Nebraska, I erupted. I pulled to the side of the road, walked to the middle of a deserted cornfield, grabbed my paper and pen and frantically wrote a letter to God.

"...Fine, you want to take him? Take him! I don't care anymore. I have had it with "holding the balance," using the violet flame, healing light and protective bubbles. They no longer make sense. I just want to let it go and let someone else do it for awhile. Let my guidance protect me and carry me for awhile. I have had enough. What about me, God? What about me? I did as you

asked. I gave up my home, was willing to go to places never before seen, to offer the work you inspired me to bring forth. Yet, I am met by opposition. I feel so cynical about everything. It all seems so meaningless and stupid and without purpose!

Something has come over my heart, God, and I just can't afford to care anymore. I am too tired to be angry. I don't care if he stays or if he goes. There is this apathy that covers my attachment to everything. My heart feels coated with Teflon. I don't want to be moved by anything—Grandfather Sun, Sunsets, the river, Max, the Angels, the Light, even my own despair. There is no one I want to call or see. I don't care what I eat, if my body is in shape. I have lost my drive and my ambition. Everything I do is an effort, without a valued result. I don't feel vital, needed, missed, essential...My passion is once again dead...!"

When I was done, I put my pen and paper down and sighed—a sigh of relief. When I was quiet enough to listen I heard a still, gentle voice reply:

"...Cathryn, you lose hope because you are no longer in control. The outcome is unknown. There are too many variables, and you have spent your life trying to orchestrate and guide, instead of allow. But this is out of your control.

Max will get better if he chooses to get better. If he goes, it is because it is his time to go, not because you have failed. If he stays; it is his decision as well. Your hovering is cheating him of that choice."

"But what about being a co-creator? What purpose does this apathy serve? I want grace, not false hope or control."

"Well, then, let it unfold. And remember, between attachment and detachment true compassion lies. Max has not made his decision, but despite his choice, you do not fail or succeed. Your task is simply to stay open and deal with your life as it presently unfolds..."

I thought about those words. I thought about my life and reflected on its quality at that time. I was uncomfortable with what I had become. I felt caught in such an odd place—so removed from the every day world within which most reside, with its lunches and cocktails and the 9 to 5's.

How was I ever going to fit in again? I was living in this little capsule, driving around the country, completely unattached. I didn't know how to relate anymore. It was hard to be around friends. I maintained a distance and isolated out of fear. I had nothing to say to people. My work was so intense that few could understand. And who wanted to hear about Max and the trials I faced with him day to day. Most thought I was insane for holding on and not just putting him down. Even I had to wonder, why was I holding on? Was I doing it for my convenience or because Max deserved every chance to heal? His condition had gotten so bad; I wondered if there really was any hope. He was in diapers, we couldn't go for our daily runs—the quality of his life and mine had been drastically altered.

It just did not seem time to intervene. I continuously faced the possibility of miracles in the losses of letting go, testing my willingness to surrender, yet staying open and involved; demanding that I "maximize" each moment, attain and reach the highest potential of each and every moment...then relax and let that moment go. Often the test was more than I could master. It became easier to maintain a false sense of control.

A few days passed and the time came to leave for Minneapolis. I didn't want to go. It took great effort to pull the despairing parts of me along. They lingered, and sabotaged, and just simply did not want to go.

I wouldn't have even gone up north, but work was the only relief I had from the pain. It was the only avenue left for connecting to the Divine. Every other road was in desperate need of repair.

-----CHAPTER SEVEN-----

"The Dark Night of the Tour"

It was my first night in Minneapolis. Anticipating a greatly needed night of sleep, I snuggled comfortably into the "motor-home" version of a bed, but then Max began to moan. He was in pain. I climbed out of bed to go check on him.

"...Blood is dripping all over the floor. I call 411 and frantically ask for the number of an emergency animal hospital. The operator hurriedly responds to my hysteria. She finds the number of an all night animal clinic. I call for directions and discover it is only five miles away. I carry Max to the car and drive as quickly as I can on unfamiliar streets to an address unknown. Finally, I see the flashing neon sign. I quickly park and rush Max inside. We are met by a nurse who leads us to an examination room. The doctor on duty examines Max and immediately catheterizes him. It is all he can do...I am handed a bill for sixty-three dollars and sent on my way..."

We returned to the home of the stranger who had graciously agreed to let Max and I hook up the RV; I tried to be quiet. I did not want to awaken my new host. I placed Max on the bed and made a cup of hot tea. The bleeding was in check, but Max continued to moan.

"...I hold Max in my arms and rock him back and forth. I wonder if he will make it through the night. My heart is heavy and I feel very, very alone. It has been a long time since I felt such loneliness or the longing for comfort from another human being. My despair had camouflaged that need; such longings had been met by turning to the Divine. But tonight I need human comfort. Yet, I know not a soul in Minneapolis, not one person to whom I can turn for support..."

In the darkness of the night, entrenched in the depth of my need, my heart began to stir. It was softening. My loneliness had penetrated the shell of my apathy. It was inviting me to once again feel pain. The threat of losing Max had reawakened my need for human contact. It had set the stage for my wounded heart to heal. I was once again experiencing a desire and a need to trust. Without the threat of losing Max, I may have never become receptive to taking that kind of risk again.

Fortunately, God placed someone on my path who was worthy of such trust. Dr. Winter is a holistic Veterinarian in Uptown Minneapolis. He was the first Vet who treated me with dignity. He suggested we operate. It was the only way we could accurately assess the situation and determine what course to pursue. Dr. Winter did warn me, however, that I could lose Max on the operating table. He also cautioned that we could discover that the illness was so progressed that it would necessitate putting Max to sleep right on the spot. The alternative was to treat him homeopathically and see what happened.

I needed time to think. Max and I went and sat by one of the lakes. I had to prepare us for the possibility that these hours may be the last that we would share. I have never felt more alone. Not even the night before matched the depth of aloneness I felt in those moments by the lake. I was in a strange city with not one friend in sight.

Although it had its risks, I decided to go through with the operation. I had to know the full scope of the situation. Dr. Winter invited me to observe the operation. It was the only way I could have coped. I knew—and he knew—that if Max expired, I had to be there.

"...Dr. Winter and his assistant begin to prepare for the operation. Max is given the anesthesia. I sit on the stairs. Frightened, I hold my hand to my own heart. Its steady beat keeps me calm and grounded. My eyes focus on the rising and falling of Max's chest. I pray he just keeps breathing. Dr. Winter cuts into Max's belly. Drops of blood splatter onto his freshly pressed shirt. The bladder is finally exposed. Its walls are severely hardened. It is this that causes the bleeding. The

kidneys look weak. The only clue that there has been a tumor is the remnants of scar tissue that remain attached to the walls of the bladder. It appears as though it has successfully been dissolved. Everything else looks healthy, in no need of repair.

Having seen what he needed to see, Dr. Winter instructs his assistant to sew Max up. He turns to me with a hopeful glance then suggests I wait for Max upstairs. I ask if it is possible for me to remain by his side. He agrees with a nod and a smile then asks his assistant to provide me with a chair. I position myself next to Max's sleeping body. I rest my hand on his paw and wait the three hours it takes for him to begin to stir. Once awake, we carry him to the car. I drive back to the RV..."

Max has survived the operation; there is once again hope. The next morning Max and I returned to Dr. Winter's. We had to start treating his bladder walls in an attempt to "soften" them so they could expand and contract as the bladder filled and then released. The bladder is the organ that holds fear. It is my belief that Max's hardened bladder was a metaphor for my hardened heart. There was a parallel between the two...both had to heal so they could properly fill and release with ease.

We used herbs to soften the walls of Max's bladder. The softening agent for my heart was my work. It was the only other role which strengthened my will to stay open. Instead of dreading the last leg of the tour, as I had several days earlier, I now found myself feeling excited about beginning with this new class. It was a group of all women. I liked mixed groups, but somehow the feminine energy promised a unique challenge. They were ready and eager to work, to share and to make movement in the resolution of their pain.

Even my renewed enthusiasm could not outweigh the fatigue. I was wearing down. The ordeal with Max resulted in one crisis after another, the bleeding; the clotting; the blockage; the anemia; the urinating two to three times an hour. I needed to work, and yet, I felt like the mother of a newborn babe. I seldom slept. I was up every other minute letting Max out to urinate. It seemed as though things never settled down enough for Max to get ahead. And I was sleep-deprived, depressed and still lonelier than I had ever been.

One morning I awakened to a stomach full of panic. I felt trapped, with nowhere to run. I meditated, prayed and asked God to please help me survive the next wave of grief that was about to crash through the shores of my exhaustion, loneliness and despair.

"...A voice whispers in my ear "Cathryn, you are not alone." Blue and pink flames descend and commingle to form a radiant, violet flame. The flame gently wraps itself around Max and lifts him high into the sky where things are pure and without density.

The Healing Circle is again summoned. Sue, Alyssa, Anna Maria, Darlene, Greg, Walter, Dr. Winter, Tim, Joy, and Mother Mary position themselves in a circle around Max and me. Max's head rests in my lap. My hand rests on his forehead. Jesus comes forward and once again gives Max a transfusion of light. The bladder is coated with a beautiful softening gel, which soothes and seals. In unison, the circle begins to chant. They continue until Max returns to a state of health. In the world of the unseen, Max is in perfect health, his bladder control has returned. He now has free choice to stay or go. The scene fades from my mind and I am left in a state of absolute awe..."

Each time I experienced a healing meditation such as this I was able to let go of Max a little bit more. Nonetheless, it was difficult to stay out of his way, to give him the "gift" of free choice. It was hard to give up control. The meditations felt lovely, inspiring, even uplifting, and yet, there was this nagging voice inside who was not so eager to concede.

I was unsure of how to quiet this voice, the one who had run the show for so long. She only knew how to respond, control, fix and hold onto the hope for change. I was willing to let go, but was she? I didn't know how strong I had to get before I could secure the reins. What I did know, however, was that when this part of me seized center stage, I was at the mercy of her whims.

When I was not struggling to stay in control I was fighting despair. I wrote to a friend,

"...At night, when my last student leaves and I close the door to the RV, I enter a whole different world...a form of my own hell. I look for comfort, but there is none. Food has little appeal. TV irritates. Phone calls

exaggerate the distance and emptiness I feel inside. My body has no more will to work out. All sources of pleasure have vanished. When I look to Max—I quickly turn away. I don't want him to absorb any more of my pain or my despair.

I am without answers. I have no more questions to ask. Yet, I keep looking for some sign. Each morning I awake wondering if he will still be alive. My next thought is 'Do I want him to be?' I don't know how much more of his suffering I can bear. But what are the options? To put him to sleep so it is over? When and if I feel directed to do this, I will. Until that time, I will do whatever I need to do to support him in making the decision. Making the decision for him does not seem like a choice, but getting through tomorrow and the next day seems like such a chore..."

An aspect of my dilemma demanded that I grieve not just what my life would be without Max, but what it had indeed become. What I grieved most was our morning runs. Every time I put on my track shoes his tail began to wag. If I walked out of the RV without him, he barked as if to say, "What about me?" One day I gave in to his pleading eyes and attempted to take him for a short run. He collapsed even before we made it out of the driveway. I brought him back into the RV and began to face the fact that much of the life we had shared was gone. That thought shattered my heart in two.

I sat around for the next few days and did not run. That didn't work either. Running is my stabilizer. When

I do not run, I get even more depressed. I had little enthusiasm, but I was forced to reconcile the fact that my physical activity had to carry on without Max. The biggest challenge however, was reconciling the release of our symbiotic tie. It involved a willingness and an ability to process the many stages of grief; to embrace the shock and panic, my need to bargain, my anger and despair. This challenge was dramatically illuminated the last day of the class—the day we were to focus on their childhood grief.

-----CHAPTER EIGHT-----

"The Grueling Clutch of Grief"

It was Grief Day, the day of the workshop dedicated to working with the exercises and ceremonies of the five stages of grief. Max was tied up outside. He was not doing well. The Vet had instructed me to watch for symptoms of anemia. If his gums turned too light and if he vomited, I was to call the hospital immediately.

We had just completed the exercises for the first few stages of grief—panic, denial and bargaining. The next set of exercises dealt with the stage of anger, resentment and rage. Max began to bark. A participant checked on him and motioned that I should come and look for myself. He had thrown up. I checked his gums; they looked almost white. I called the hospital and the nurse advised me to bring him in so they could examine him and assess if he needed an I.V.

I explained the situation to the class and asked if we could break early for lunch. I knew I could not continue to facilitate the exercises with this crisis unresolved. They came through like champs.

"...My anxiety is running high. I rush Max to the Emergency Veterinary Hospital. The nurse looks at his mouth, then turns to me and says, "He looks just fine." Tears of embarrassment and relief rush from my throat to my eyes down my cheeks. I blurt out, "But what about his vomiting? And aren't his gums too white?" She looks again and replies that he must have eaten some grass that caused the regurgitation and his gums look a little pale, but not so light that he is at risk.

I become hysterical and begin to babble on and on..."This is too much! I have lost all perspective. I have become so obsessed with my dog's symptoms that I am severely compromising my work. I have a class of women waiting for me to proceed, but how I can teach them about their grief when I have so much of own to bear!" The nurse, without judgment, recommends I leave Max with her for the rest of the day.

I turn to Max and explain what is going to occur. I assure him it has nothing to do with him...that I am unable to keep my focus on work because I am so worried about his condition. He licks my face to tell me good-bye. I turn and leave.

I get behind the wheel of my car and again burst into tears. This time they are tears of anger. It angers me that I am so overly concerned. I am exasperated. I clasp onto the steering wheel in desperation and pray to be shown what to do. With great frustration, I begin to pound on the wheel. Sobs of angry protest get unleashed. Finally, the tears begin to subside. So does the anger. I feel the comfort of the Light as it fills *the space no longer occupied by my anger and my despair..."*

Before I could facilitate the exercises on anger I had to voice my own. And when I did, God had listened with an open ear.

My anger was gone, but I still felt ill at ease. It frightened me that there was so little distance between my personal life and my work-related responsibilities. It left me feeling incredibly vulnerable.

I took a deep breath and then returned to the class. I led them through the remaining exercises with a sense of calm. We then went to the river and did our ceremonies of release. When we returned for the potluck, we sat in circle for closure. After each had shared what they needed to share, I related the experience I had had that day. I apologized for any distress I may have caused them and disclosed how difficult the last several weeks had been. It felt risky to disclose. Yet...they deserved some explanation. I could not always be as together as I would have liked to have been. At least I could hold myself accountable for my actions and offer an explanation as to why I felt I fell short of what they deserved.

Their response was like warm milk and cookies. Again, I was shown so much love, understanding and appreciation for being honest, open and real. It was a true gift from Spirit, delivered through the eyes and words of these women with whom I had had the honor to work.

I went to pick up Max. The nurse said he had done fine. We went back to the river. As we relaxed on the banks of the Mississippi, something inside let go, and as it did, the next layer of grief emerged. On the other side of the anger was a new form of fear—a fear laced with extreme sadness at seeing Max deteriorate before my very eyes. While the bleeding had diminished and his anemia was under control; his legs could no longer support him. His condition was getting worse.

Later that day Max was resting on the bed. I went and lay down next to him. My consciousness immediately swirled up into a meditative state. I heard this voice say, "Max has decided to make his transition." It was very strange...it wasn't the cat energy this time. There was a different quality about this message. I jumped off that bed like I had seen a ghost. The experience scared me and forced me to face the fact that Max may choose to leave.

I had been giving voice to my desire to allow Max to make his own decision. But on a deeper level, I still believed he would choose to stay. After all we had been through, I could not fathom the possibility he would choose to leave. I didn't want to lose him. I wanted us to run together and celebrate our initiation together. It had been such a long journey. I didn't want it to end with having to say good bye to him. I wanted him to accompany me to my next destination, to be present for the final healing of my heart.

I was disturbed. It was like an omen, a message, and I was having a hard time accepting it. I just could not comprehend why, when given the opportunity to stay,

Max would choose to go. I hated to admit it, but it brought up an even deeper set of feelings. It was time to write another letter to God.

"...God, I feel like I always hang in there with others one hundred percent. I do whatever I need to do to stay open. I do not leave. I am always the one who is left—the one who has to deal with abandonment. Just once, can't all of my efforts pay off? I want someone, just once, to choose to stay around—to confront what he or she needs to confront so they will not have to leave or turn away. No matter what I do it seems as though everyone always ends up leaving me. Does this have to be true even of Max...?"

I knew how lethal that state of victimization could become. I had to deal with it before it got out of hand. I did not want to project any guilt onto Max. I felt frantic. I knew I had to get out of the RV for awhile. My feelings were too intense to be around him. I went back and told Max I was going to go for a ride. I leaned down to be near him and then explained that some pretty ugly feelings were coming up. I needed to be alone. I had started talking to him like I would a person. I figured it couldn't hurt. I believed a part of him understood what I was saying.

I walked out of the RV and began to drive. I took a breath, surrounded myself and the car in Light and began to scream and shout. Every feeling of abandonment and betrayal finds its expression through my tears. Most are familiar, feelings previously addressed in some other time and space. Then I hear myself scream a feeling of which I was totally unaware.

"I can't believe, Max, after all I have done for you that you, that you would still choose to leave!!!"

The truth of this statement touches me to the very bone.

I realized, for the first time, that this feeling was the foundation of every major relationship I had ever had. I was always "doing for others" in hopes they would stay. But I now saw that it was all done with a price, a condition, an expectation of a promise that they would never leave. It was my co-dependent bargain. I had developed it early in relationship to Dad. "I will take care of you in hopes that you will turn around and make me feel safe." Of course, it would have to emerge in this ordeal with Max. It was one of the main layers of feelings I had to confront if I were to heal my own heart. This pattern carried my blueprint of intimacy—the legacy I had learned in my relationship to Dad.

It felt good to finally reach the bottom of my resentment, to see the patterns of conditionality and how they related to my treatment of Max. Once I could admit to these feelings, I began to dialogue with the part of me who carried this theme. As I did, I was able to attain a peacefulness with respect to Max's inevitable choice.

I drove back to the RV. As soon as I walked in the door Max started to whine, as though summoning me. I went to him but could not figure out what he wanted. I couldn't tell if he wanted food, or water or needed his diaper changed. Finally, I leaned over and said, "Honey, I just don't know what you want." When I got close enough he started to lick my face. He licked and licked and licked, like he knew what I had just experienced and was thanking me for moving into this new state of unconditionality. It was one of the most affectionate and intimate moments of my life.

I was beginning to see how this crisis with Max was indeed assisting me in the healing of my heart. In fact, it was forcing me to examine every layer of betrayal to which I had ever felt victim.

I had worked through the betrayal I felt in response to Max. I didn't know, however, that there was another layer of betrayal lurking below. I only knew I was agitatedly anxious. I found myself getting irritated when I had to wait in line at the grocery store, even though I had no place to go. I felt cranky when I would try to reach someone by telephone and it would ring and ring and ring. It was as if I expected others to be responsive to every need. Little signs indicated that all was not peaceful inside. I could not label it or grasp it. It was just too big to comprehend.

When I felt betrayed by those who "left me," I simply severed the relationships, claiming it was the only way to keep my integrity intact. But I could have never guessed I felt betrayed by the Source of my highest faith. To feel betrayed by God, when I was two thousand miles away from the arms of a friend, living in a traveling home with no address or phone, on a mission *inspired* by God, how could I feel angry and betrayed by that very Source? Severing my trust in the relationship with God would have dissolved the very foundation upon which I had based my whole tour. I couldn't admit I felt angry and betrayed. There was way too much to lose. The problem was that this was exactly what I felt—angry and betrayed by God.

-----CHAPTER NINE-----

"A Witness for My Rage"

The phone rings. It is my friend, Alyssa who has been in my life for almost a decade. We often stand witness to the expression of each other's pain. She is one to whom I can say anything. I know it is safe to speak to her about my rage at God with no fear. She assists me in speaking my truth, tells me she is willing to be a witness for my rage

"Say what you really need to say. Get it all out."

And so I did. I did with Alyssa what I had been helping others all over the country do when they uncovered their hidden rage. In the presence of a witness I gave voice to the part of me who so badly needed to speak and to be heard.

I ranted and I raved.

"...I am out there doing my life's work and all I asked for in return was to be able to have Max journey with me and to have the classes well-attended. How could you, God, mess with my primary source of safety? I

*GAVE UP MY HOME, MY FRIENDS, STEADY EMPLOY-
MENT, AND PREDICTABILITY. All I wanted in return
was well-attended classes and the companionship of
Max to remain secure. Was that too much to expect?!?"*

When all had not turned out as I had hoped, I was
angry with God, but I could not admit to that anger. It
left me feeling too alone, too wrong, too vulnerable and
afraid.

I had become more and more tense, more and more
focused on Max's healing, my next meal, making sure
there was oil in the car—anything that would keep my
attention away from the rage.

Now there was too much emotional charge to keep
the intensity caged. I had become so fatigued that my
protective façade finally shattered and my anger
leaked through the splinters of my vulnerability. I
could no longer contain feeling betrayed by God. I was
too exhausted from trying to make it work. I didn't
care where the chips would fall if the rage was set
loose. I felt betrayed and the voice that carried that
feeling could no longer be silenced. Right or wrong, it
could no longer go without having its say.

As I am screaming my protestations, I look up. Max
catches my glance.

*"...His tail is wagging. He stares me right in the eye.
"But I was never part of the bargain. I agreed to come
on this journey on my own. This is not your cancer, it is
mine. It is not your recovery, it is mine..."*

I froze—became mute. Alyssa asked what has just occurred.

When my speech returned, I described what had happened. I began to talk about how afraid I was to be on the journey alone. I had taken responsibility for Max's illness. I was willing to heal **anyone's** pain if it meant they would not leave me. I did the same with Dad. I took on his depression in hopes that I could heal him enough so he would not have to be distant and depressed.

I sobbed and sobbed. I felt pathetic, ashamed and exposed. But it felt good to speak my ugly truth and wonderful to have such a dear friend.

In that moment, having had the courage to embrace my anger at God, the force of my wrath dissolved. I began to see how God had not let me down. My classes had been filled with participants and my pockets filled with cash. I had been given the time and the resources to do what needed to be done with respect to Max. Greg had once said that the decision to go on this journey was my agreement with God—Max was not a part of that agreement. I realized how true his words really were.

Once again I embraced the fact that Max might decide to heal and stay, or he might decide his time on earth was complete. Each layer of grief demanded that I wrestle with, and adjust to, the discomfort of that unknown.

I realized when the Angels directed me to say to Max, "You do what you need to do. My commitment to you is to provide for you and assist you beyond my own needs..." that I had not really grasped what they actually meant and the price that that vow would indeed take.

We all say words to which we want to adhere, but seldom do we understand what it really means to live up to what we say.

I did a ceremony in which I expressed my gratitude to Max for his willingness to play his part, and I sat down to finally write an apology to God.

"...God, I am sorry I held you responsible for Max's illness. I realize I made a bargain that could not be sealed because it was a bargain that involved Max's life. His life is not a bargaining chip I have a right to use. I can honor his life, and hold it sacred, but it is not mine to use. Please assist me in moving to the next step with this. Please assist me in making my amends..."

After this episode I had to bring my attention back to work. I had to decide if I were going to extend my stay. Plans to travel to the Northwest had been canceled. There had, however, been some interest in my offering another, shorter version of the Intensive in Minneapolis. I had a few days before I had to make up my mind, so I prayed for some sign as to whether to stay or go.

-----CHAPTER TEN-----

"A Toss of a Coin Determines Our Fate"

The several days passed. It was time to make a decision about the next few weeks. Still ambivalent, I asked for a more definite sign. Spirit gave me one clue. I had barely mentioned the possibility of offering a ten-day Mini-Workshop. Nonetheless, I had already received a deposit. It was the one indication I had that I was to follow through with the plan to stay. Most thought I was nuts. They advised me to pack up and go—but go where? I had no idea what was going to happen. But I was also not sure if I had the tenacity to work for two more weeks.

The only way I could make the decision was to completely turn it over to God. I took some of the Inner Child herbs that Sue, an herbalist and a friend, had prepared for me, I added to this the deposit, a check made out by an Arthur Anczarski—the only tangible clue I had that I was to extend my stay and offer this additional class. I reached for my lucky wheat back penny and knew, with one toss, the fate of the next two weeks would be told. If it landed on tails, I would stay. If it were heads, I would make my arrangements to go!

The penny landed and then rolled. When it came to a rest, it was tails.

I turned to Max and said, "Ok, Max, I guess this Arthur Anczarski has the deciding vote. We stay in Minneapolis for two more weeks."

I thought to myself, "Yes, this is definitely a mature way to make a decision such as this!!" I glanced back at Max and wondered to myself if he would even be around in two weeks.

Once the decision was made I called the coordinator and asked her to go ahead and make the necessary arrangements. I felt relieved that I still had a few days to myself. I badly needed the break.

On the night I started the Mini-Workshop, I prayed I had made the right decision. The class felt great. Then again, I hadn't had a group that did not feel receptive and good. Arthur came and introduced himself to me. I shook his hand and told him that I remembered his name from this list. I thought to myself, "Ha! If he only knew how instrumental he had been in my staying."

I was still not sure if extending my stay had been the best decision with respect to Max. I tried to remind myself of something Dr. Winter had said—that it was common in chronic illnesses to have good and bad days. If Max took a turn for the worse, I could not control it or change it. All I could do was love him and hold the part within me who wanted to control. I needed to teach her that these ups and downs were just life, the ebb and flow of life. Some days are great and inspirational. Others are merely mundane.

The last day of any of these workshops was always challenging for the participants, but this one was also difficult for me. I had my own grief with which to contend. It was the last scheduled event of the tour. It had been a long journey. I had been on the road for a year, moving from city to city, establishing a meaningful connection with others and then leaving town. I had nursed a very sick dog through a very hard illness. He was still with me, but I knew in my heart that it would be his last journey as well.

When I had closure with the class, my eyes welled up with tears. I was not only saying good-bye to this group, but to the many groups that had gone before them.

That night I had dinner with the one friend I had met in Minneapolis. He is a trained Shaman. There was an instant rapport with Timothy. He was another one of the angels that God had sent to me. That night he was conducting a shamanic drumming circle. I decided to attend. It felt good to attend a gathering where I could participate instead of facilitate. I desperately needed the support.

And it was healing to hear the beating of the drums.

The next day was the final consultation with the individuals who had participated in the class. Arthur's appointment was the last one of the day. After we had completed the consultation discussing what he had learned in the Intensive, we began to talk as friends.

There was a familiarity that we both felt...a recognition of each other that suggested we had indeed known each other in another time and place. That had been one of the gifts of this whole journey—the gift of crossing paths with souls along the way who held the familiarity of old-time friends and acquaintances from forgotten times gone by. Nonetheless, fatigue caught up with us and it came time to go our separate ways. We bid our farewells then promised to stay in touch.

Those last few days in Minneapolis had been full of many mixed emotions. The last night was particularly difficult. I awoke at 4:30 a.m. I couldn't sleep. I felt unsettled...anxious to get back home yet, sad to leave. I was full of the experiences I had had while in Minneapolis. I was inspired by the work and the new ideas, but drained from the stress with Max.

I arrived in Nebraska and looked forward to relaxing for a week before I had to return to California. It felt good to be on familiar ground. The trip had been long and tedious. It made me realize how stressful the last year had been and how badly I needed to settle somewhere and assimilate all that had been laid on my path since going on the road. I could not help but wonder how the adventure would have been different had I not had to deal with the episodic crises with Max. Even with that wonderment, I never doubted the value of all of the trials and tribulations, the most challenging of which was about to take place.

-----CHAPTER ELEVEN-----

"The Beginning of the End Has Begun"

The drive to Nebraska took longer than planned. The tour was over. The mission was complete. I had no place I needed to be except a routine dental appointment scheduled months before in an attempt to take care of the basics before I returned to California and began anew. I had little zip left. I was worn out and could not be rushed.

"...Running late, I hurriedly park the RV and dash inside. Max waits patiently in our traveling home, parked once again, in unfamiliar surroundings.

The assistant leads me back to the examination room and tells me the doctor will be in soon. Dr. Stec greets me with a smile, lowers the chair, pokes around in my mouth, deadens my gums, then leaves.

Sitting quietly in that dental chair with no distractions, I, unexpectedly, begin to weep. Something tells me that the time has come to finally let Max go. There are no new symptoms. There is just something inside of my belly that intuitively knows the time has simply come.

For an instant I wonder if this sudden outburst signals that the time is indeed already here. Has it perhaps already happened? Is Max waiting for me to find him at his final resting-place on the front seat of the RV?

The Dentist walks back into the room. The Novocain has sufficiently deadened my mouth as well as the tears. I don't think about it again until we get back to my mother's home. It is mid-afternoon. The local vet is familiar with the situation. I call him and ask if I can bring Max down for an examination. He had run some tests on him six weeks earlier. The vet duplicates the tests and says he will call.

It is late in the afternoon. The tests indicate that my earlier intuition carried the truth. Max's system is indeed poisoning him. His kidneys are severely compromised. His bladder walls are too hard to flex adequately enough for Max to release. We talk about options. There are few..."

I grabbed Max and lifted him into Mom's truck. I was in a trance—but I needed to move—go for a drive—find someplace where I could think this out.

When the truck finally came to a stop I found myself out at the local cemetery, parking next to Dad's grave.

Since his death I had not had a great attachment to the grave. I felt such a connection with him on the other side that his grave did not seem that significant to me. But on that day I was naturally drawn to this site.

"...I park the truck. Max and I get out. I sit on the ground and lean against a bench that my sister, brothers and I had purchased and had placed at the foot of Dad's grave. Max scouts around then finds his way to my lap. I encircle his body with my legs. He falls into a deep, deep sleep, relaxing for the first time in months. I stroke his head and let myself relax as well. It is the first time I am ready to really embrace the truth that the beginning of the end had begun..."

For more than eight years we had been each other's best friend, and in the last few years we had seldom been apart. With the on going connection with Greg, and the help of Dr. Winter, Max had managed to hang on until we completed our tour. Now, sensing that our work was done, he could finally begin to let go.

"...The moment is cosmic. Birds sing in the background. The wind gently brushes my face. I feel the warmth of Grandfather Sun, almost as if his hand is on my shoulder, offering me badly needed support.

I tell Max all that he had meant to me. I tell him what he can expect when the time actually comes for him to release. I use the pendulum to check out Max's energy and to obtain the answers I need in order to know how to proceed.

I telepathically explain to Max how we will call in the angels and how the wild dogs, which had helped him in his healing, have also offered to attend. I tell him that Master Wolf has offered to preside over the transition and that the healing team has agreed to convene once more.

I share what I envision for him in his next phase. And I assure him (and me) that although we will not be together in the physical sense he can be with me in the spiritual realm whenever he feels the need..."

I reflected on when I had had a similar conversation with Dad almost six years before this. It was odd that I now sat at Dad's grave talking to the being with which I had shared my most private moments of the last several years about his transition as well.

It suddenly became apparent that I wanted to assist Max with his transition on that very spot.

I knew it would be an odd request especially back in my small, Midwestern hometown. It was not California or the Southwest where such requests were considered a little more natural. I knew, even if this event was not newsworthy enough to make it into the local paper, it would nevertheless make the rounds.

But I was committed to completing our time together in the same manner in which we had lived it—with reverence and ceremony.

By the grace of God, I hooked up with a new vet in town who had worked in the Southwest, and even though I was quite shy about my inquiries, he was very supportive and understanding of my wishes. Dr. Lonti was more than willing to meet me at Dad's grave if that was what I chose. We agreed to meet the following Thursday at noon. I wanted the procedure to take place right at noon when Grandfather Sun would be the most direct, so Max could follow the beam of sunlight straight to the Divine.

I spent those next few days talking with Max about the event, preparing him for what was about to take place. At first Max seemed squeamish about the idea of an injection. He didn't know if it was going to hurt. He didn't know what it all meant.

And I battled with my own ambivalence.

I didn't want to have Max put to sleep for my convenience. By the same token I did not want to keep Max alive to avoid my feelings of loss either.

The last few days were very difficult. I talked with friends and trusted advisors. And, of course, I talked with Max.

I was at odds with the prospect of intervening. It felt like a contradiction to now consider being so instrumental in his death. I had struggled so much in those last few months with letting go and allowing the course of Max's treatment to be in his hands and not mine. Greg was helpful. He sensed Max was really tired; noticing a difference in Max's energy just since we left Minnesota. He comforted me by saying the he believed if Max were out in nature he would simply go somewhere, find a comfortable place and curl up to die. But Max was domesticated and needed my help to be put to rest.

Max and I spent time together in silence; in denial; in communion. Yet the gut-wrenching pain in the pit of my stomach was never far away. At unexpected moments, I would feel it rise within me, regurgitating the feelings of companionship to which I needed to bid farewell. Tears welled up in my eyes, followed by a lump in my throat; soon the nauseous feeling of loss would command release.

The decision to put Max to sleep was never really consciously made—it simply evolved as each piece fit together and ultimately led to the planning of the sacred event.

In the next few days we spent a lot of our time at the cemetery. I wanted to give Max's spirit as much time as possible to get familiar with the surroundings from which it would leave and prepare the ground (and us) for what was soon to take place. Max was comfortable there. Each time we went, he would not want to leave. It was like he knew it would be the place he would find his peace. I, too, found comfort at Dad's grave. I could feel Dad's presence as well as the presence of the many helpers from the unseen.

We went on Wednesday and ceremoniously prepared the space. We called in the four directions, summoned the healing team, and chose the music and poems we wanted to use. I respectfully placed an offering of liver treats in the four directions to pay honor to the spirit animals that would preside. Max had his own way of showing his respect. He promptly consumed the treats behind my back. It was a nice touch of the familiar. His spirit was not completely gone!

I then held Max on my lap while I played the songs and poems for him. The next time he would hear them he would have already gone to the other side.

Each day was filled with its odds and ends...its good-byes...its tears. But nothing compared to our last night.

It was one of the most emotionally tumultuous nights of my life.

I was losing the main source of security I had in the physical realm. It was like standing on quick sand, which was always moving, altering my stability. Every fear, every loss, every fiber of insecurity knocked on my door that night—all demanding expression and release.

I spent time reflecting on the life Max and I had shared. I recalled again our initial initiation over which Master Wolf had presided. Max had indeed become my healer. No one could soften my heart more than Max. Except for the few I had met on the tour, Max was the only being who had touched it in years.

Max seemed to sense his job was complete. I was opening up and beginning to trust again. I do not know what I would have done that last night without my newfound friend, Arthur. We talked on the phone for several hours. I don't recall the subject of our conversation; I just remember not wanting to hang up. I didn't want to face the night alone. In the end, no one could rescue me from that emptiness and fear, not even my newfound friend.

Max had a hard night as well. He was restless and in pain. I could feel his spirit wandering, searching for its next home. One time I had my head close to his belly and I could literally hear this deep elemental cry within him begging for relief. It dissolved any ambivalence I had about the decision. It did not, however, ease the pain of the ensuing loss.

-----CHAPTER TWELVE-----

"It Is Time to Say Good-bye"

The night was long. I tossed. I turned. I finally fell asleep.

I am awakened by the spirit of Lillian, my little Godchild and Max's dear friend. She tapped me on the shoulder and said she has come to kiss Max good-bye. It was sweet and very real.

That moment passed. I become engulfed by the dread of what must now take place. With a sense of urgency, I checked on Max. He'd made it through the night. I swallowed the tears that accompany the thought of this being the last morning such a greeting will take place. But it was too early for tears. I knew I would never make it through the day if the tears began this soon.

I meditate, take a bath, and then began the final preparations.

I filled the truck with the Indian drum and flute, the tapes, the sage, and the teddy bear that represented my own inner child—the little girl inside who also had to say good-bye. We left far too early to go the cemetery. I instinctively drove to the family farm to check on the land. It was a trip I had often made with Dad when I was a child. One I now made with my brother anytime I was home for a visit.

I drove on the country roads where Max and I had so often run, to the river, where I sat and played my drum. We then made our way to the cemetery—Dad's, and soon to be Max's, final resting-place.

"...It is a beautiful day. The wind is gentle. Grandfather Sun is shining bright...I set things up once again acknowledging the four directions and calling in the healing team. Jesus, Mother Mary, and friends, who had helped along the way, all convene one more time to assist Max in his transition to the other side.

Then, we just relax. I play the Indian drum or listen to the sounds of the Indian flute. I play a song for Dad that I had composed for him while on the road. I go over things with Max again. We talk more about the cremation and the possibilities that exist for him on the other side.

A sacred stone, clutched in the palm of my hand, connects me calmly with Mother Earth. It is a peaceful time...everything has been said and done. When Dr. Lonti arrives we are ready to proceed. It is time to say good-bye.

I call Max over to the rug he knows so well. I stroke his head and tell him all will be fine, and then I hold his leg as the vet injects the drug that will release him from his pain. Within 10 seconds his brain is asleep. Within 40 seconds, his heart has stopped its beat.

Dr. Lonti squeezes my hand in recognition of my loss. It is a greatly appreciated gesture..."

Once Dr. Lonti left I closed my eyes and placed my palms on the breathless back of Max's body. Without warning, I felt Max lick me on the side of my face. It was the strangest thing. His energy was so real—it was hard to compute he was no longer in physical form, that he was really dead. Then, again, in my mind's eye, I saw him dancing around so free and vibrant and energetic. My heart burst into happiness. My eyes filled with joyful tears. It was so wonderful to see Max pain-free.

I then saw him running around with several other dogs, playing and having fun. The others dogs had come to escort him to the other side. He looked back at me once and barked his bark that signaled he wanted me to come. I smiled, motioned for him to go on, and explained it was a trail I could not yet take. I watched as he disappeared into the Light.

I stayed at the gravesite for an hour or so...and then, because it was hot, I put Max's body in the truck until I could take it back to the clinic for the crema-tion. It was several hours before Dr. Lonti would be able to meet; but it was important to me that he and I put Max's body in the crematorium together. We had been the ones who had set him free. I wanted to keep the intervention as pure and as simple as possible. I wasn't sure how to pass the time so I ended up just riding around town with the air conditioner blowing cool air on my face and on Max's hollow body. Now, riding around in a small town in Nebraska with the dead body of your pet in the front seat was weird...even for me...it was weird.

At first the body was limp so it just seemed like Max was sleeping. But then it started to stiffen. All I could do was laugh, as I heard this voice inside say, "Well, here's another fine mess you have gotten us into!!"

I was committed, however, to stay with the body until it could be put into the crematorium. It wouldn't have felt right to go drop it off at the animal clinic and pick up the ashes later. I had to see this process through to completion. I had made a promise to Max. It was a promise I had no choice but to keep.

At one point I thought to check the pendulum to see if Max's spirit was along for the ride. But the pendulum did not move. I knew at that moment that Max had been completely freed from his body. And I thought to myself, 'Boy! Only for someone I really loved would I spend three hours riding around in a small Midwestern town protecting the discarded body until it could properly be released.'

Why I didn't just stay at the cemetery I don't know. I guess it was just too darn hot. I had already been out there for more than four hours. Another three just seemed like too much! I couldn't imagine going back to Mom's and sitting in her house watching TV while Max's body "lay in state" in the front seat of her pick-up. (Although I did go back to Mom's to go to the bathroom! She really appreciated the fact that I had his corpse in the front seat of her pick-up! Actually, after the initial shock, she said nothing. She was pretty cool through the whole ordeal.)

Mostly, I just drove around and around and around. I went back to the country, drove to Dannebrog—a town 10 miles away—on the back roads where Max and I had once run. Then I felt inspired to drive back out to the grave site. I found myself motivated to use the pendulum again, just to see if Max's spirit was still near. Sure enough, it moved. Max had not gone far. I continued my inquiries. It felt strange communicating with the spirit of my dead dog with some rock tied to a string! Eighty percent of me thought it was nuts...absolutely, certifiably nuts. And yet, the other twenty percent knew there was something to it...knew it was as real as what I could see. Sometimes I wondered, with a smile, what side of sanity was I really walking on here!

I asked Max if he was all right. The pendulum swung "No." I asked if he were scared. It swung a strong yes. With a series of questions I was able to deduce that when I had left with the body, Max had become frightened. He was disoriented. Then a higher voice came in and explained that Max would now have to learn how to sense my vibration so that he could still be close. When I left, he was unable to detect my departure. When his spirit sensed I was gone, it had panicked just as Max may have panicked in the physical realm had he been lost.

I realized a whole new dimension had opened up. All of a sudden it seemed feasible that Max and I were still going to be able to pal around together. It would just be in a different dimension. It all felt so cosmic and mystical and yet so very real.

Although I had had a great deal of experience communicating with those in the unseen, Dad was the only other one that I had known in the physical realm as well. I didn't have a clue as to how things would evolve or what kind of contact Max and I were about to have. A whole new adventure seemed possible.

I didn't know what was in store for me...for Max and me...together and apart. I didn't know what Spirit had planned. I just knew that what died and was consumed by fire that day was the body that had so graciously served Max to the end. His spirit had been set free.

I knew there were still more tears to cry, and memories of our physical life together that would need to be grieved. But I also felt relief.

I felt such a strong presence of Max over the next few days. I had my moments of grief, but I was spending some nice time with Mom, and friends called. Plus, I was finally getting some decent sleep. I went to Lincoln the following weekend to spend some time with friends. Arthur drove down from Minneapolis that following Monday. It was great to see him. I took him to all of the spots where Max and I had gone. It was a real purging to tell him the whole story about Max and me. He was becoming a good friend and was the first new person I had been willing to trust in a very long time. I felt fortunate. Without that trust, the grief would have been too much. The door to my heart may have once again closed, slammed shut in response to the despair.

-----CHAPTER THIRTEEN-----

"Beyond the Grief"

I returned to California, put the RV in storage and rented a little cottage from a close friend. It was strange returning without Max. Going up to Mount Tamalpais was even worse. Max had always loved the mountain. One time he was so full of anticipation that he was shifting back and forth in the front seat. Somehow his nose hit the windshield and the impact cracked the glass. It was one of those $300 "Kodak" moments!

Settling into my new home without Max was also heart wrenching. I unpacked the urn that contained his ashes. Touching the bone that had held his flesh triggered a flood of tears. Tears of anger. Tears of blame. There was a battle going on within me. This time it was a battle between my personality and my Soul. Their agendas seemed so far apart.

The pain my personality had to endure because of this split erupted one day in a stream of hurtful accusations slung from my personality towards the heart of my Soul.

91

"...You are so cruel and stupid. I can not believe what you expect of me. How could you set it up so that I have to live without Max?

I want to get back at you; I want to show you that I do not have to be at your whim.

You are above the human realm of pain and loss, so what do you care. You go away at night, have your unions with God and with those you love on the other side. But I am trapped in this dimension of time. I have no escape from the pain.

I have these moments, moments when I forget that Max is gone. I listen for his bark to mark the beginning of my day much like another would listen for the sound of their alarm clock.

But for me there is no beginning!

I used to wake up to his jumping on the bed, commanding that I return immediately from my state of sleep. He had to go out. He was hungry. He was ready to start his day.

Now, no one cares if I sleep or awake. I roll from slumber into consciousness without a stir from a single soul. I hate having no one to whom I can say, "Good Morning, how did you sleep?..."

And my runs...ha!!! Each step that hits the ground giggles the grief of not having Max biting at my side and jumping at my heels. I feel as though I have a twenty-pound weight on each ankle. I have not once out run my grief...NOT ONCE!!! I always collapse into tears before I reach the end of the trail.

And still, as I drive from one place to another, I instinctively search for the most appropriate place where I can stop along the road and let him out for a stretch.

I had to go into the city last night. I involuntarily pulled into the Marina to let Max have a little walk before he would have to wait in the car. I had parked and turned the motor off before I remembered—there was no Max.

When I returned to the car, the despair was even greater. There was such an emptiness that used to be filled with his bright, welcoming eyes and his tail that wagged and confirmed his enthusiasm for my return.

And I miss his motion in the car. He use to fret between the front and the back, and then would position himself regally in the back window, as if he were standing guard over our journey.

You know how I have coped? I have put a ridiculous, life-sized, stuffed tiger in the back window. I am sure I look quite mad. But I cannot bear to look in the rear view mirror and see such emptiness.

And my leg...oh how it misses his head resting on it.

The worst is that Lillian, my Godchild, remember, the child who knew Max from the moment of her birth, she keeps asking me why I had to kill Max and cries because she cannot see him.

What do I tell her? Nothing! I am left speechless because she speaks the voice of the little kid inside me who is equally as appalled that this year had to end as it did. My inner child screams at me, "I would have never agreed to leave our home if I would have known that you were going to take him away as you did. YOU

PROMISED HE WOULD BE OK, YOU PROMISED, YOU PROMISED!!!

So you ask, Dear Soul, how do I comfort her? I hold the teddy bear in my arms; my fingers gently brush against the nametag fastened to the collar that used to be around Max's neck. I rock and I tell her I am sorry she is in such pain. I rock and the tears finally subside. And I acknowledge that one more layer of grief has been released...."

My personality had had its say with my Soul. At least I was no longer mad at God. The battle now being fought was within. The next few months I was at war. The ebb and flow of grief catapulted me through the days; each wave demanding expression and release.

One day I awoke feeling apathetic and listless. I called Darlene, my spiritual counselor, and decided to go to her for a session. It is a two and a half-hour drive, but I always enjoyed the effort it took to go to Darlene's. The energy expended made the session even that more valuable and precious. Darlene carries a wisdom that is much beyond her years. She always greeted me with warm food for my belly, arms that hugged my Soul and inspirations that enhanced my inner journey.

On the drive down I listened to a variety of recorded songs I had complied for such trips. The several songs I had played at Max's final ceremony drifted over the speakers. Within seconds I was gulping down the tears. This emotional outburst was so great that it dissolved all signs of indifference and apathy. The tears were coming from such a deep state of despair that it was almost impossible to drive.

"...I am fifty miles away from my new cottage. There are no distractions, no phone calls to make. There is just the open road and the space between my home and hers...space that mirrors my own void...filled only with the pure, unadulterated grief of beginning a new life without Max. It is like learning to exist without my left arm.

I am left-handed.

It is quite a feat..."

Each endeavor shared with Max needed to be re-learned in order to incorporate his absence. It left such an empty hole.

One distraction from the emptiness was my ever-developing friendship with Arthur. It felt good to be trusting again. Yet, opening up was also riddled with terror. The grief and the greeting seemed almost inseparable.

I spent much of the following year traveling through the feelings of my loss of Max, recuperating from the journey on the road and doing battle with my fears of opening up to someone new. Arthur began to express an interest in my work. We spent hours on the phone talking about the process of change and trans-formation, often within the context of what we were both experiencing in our respective lives. He began to assist me in my workshops by audio and video taping my sessions for further use. The friendship gave me a sense of continuity: it helped me stay anchored in present time.

It was the only sense of continuity I had because I certainly had no enthusiasm for work. I had even less for going back out on the road. I did not have to confront that possibility however, until the next fall when I received a call inviting me to offer one of my classes in the Washington, D.C. area. I was ambivalent. That ambivalence manifested in the sluggishness of the organization of the group. I had no choice but to confront it; the indecisiveness was now interfering with my work. My moratorium had to come to an end. It had gone on long enough. Somehow I had to integrate the whole experience and get my focus back on work.

I started to examine how I felt about going back out on the road. There was obviously some block, some attitude within me that was sabotaging the plans. I uncovered a voice that felt entitled. She had this chip on her shoulder, as though she were angry, but about what? It was a righteous attitude of spiritual significance and entitlement—like that of someone who now had her abuser cornered in the Light, determined to make him pay. But pay for what? And for whom was I feeling this?

I called in my protectors, Chief, the Angels, and the healing light, then proceeded to go into meditation. I asked who inside had an attitude about the workshops in D.C. Immediately it was evident that this was a continuation of the confrontation between my personality and my Soul.

"...I am met with a coldness. I try to encourage her to come forward, inviting her to speak to me about the source of her rage.

The image is blurred. At first I hear nothing. Then, without warning, she attacks with a rash of accusations and challenges.

"Fine, you want me to go to D.C.? Well you put together the workshop, and yes, I will show up. But don't expect me to put any more energy into it. I did that once, remember?? I trusted you once. Gave up everything I owned, every ounce of security I had, because I wanted to do your work. Look where that got me. And now, you want me to go back out on the road...?? Sure, but this time it will be on my terms, not yours!..."

With enough questions I began to see that the face this part of my personality wore was the one of a righteous, well defended, yet angry, adolescent.

"...I trust and give 100% to others, yet, they still betray me. Friends use me as long as they need me, then they move on. Loved ones make promises they keep only when it is convenient and useful for them to do so. Even Spirit agreed to keep Max safe if I went on the road, but he was taken from me as well.

"No more," she protests. "I will not trust again..."

I am struck by her absolute unwillingness to bend, to concede, to soften.

She is angry at my Higher Self, who, in her reality, had abused and used her. She held this attitude, and unless I addressed her pain, she was going to sabotage my friendships and career.

The inner work continued.

"...At first, I could not see her. I could just feel the cold draft of the pain. Suddenly, I saw this castle and an armored figure standing guard. As I got closer, I could see that it was she.

Clocked in steel armor, with sword in hand, she stands erect. I approach her and ask what it is that she protects. She does not reply.

I am afraid of her. It is unusual, but I actually fear her. She is determined and absolute in her position. She lets no one near her, not even me.

I retreated, and conferred with my protectors. We stood away from the castle and observed her for a moment. Then my healing team suggested that I approach her and take charge. They inform me she is protecting something of mine. I have a right to demand its return.

I approach. My stomach feels tight and rigid. I hold strong to my position. My determination becomes bigger than my fear. I walk up to her. I declare my intention to walk through those gates. "I need to see what it is that you so vehemently guard." I swing the doors open. Behind the closed doors I see my heart. It is encased in this beautiful glass box.

I turn to her. She stands with sword tilted forward and head hung down. She has conceded, but has done so with great pain.

I go to her. I raise her head. I tell her it is time to remove the armor. She shutters in fear. I insist. I begin to dismantle the metal, one piece at a time. I am appalled at what I find. She is deformed, badly bruised and burned. Her body is covered with scars. Her eyes will not meet mine, nor will mine meet hers. The scars of what she has endured are too great for either of us to acknowledge..."

Piece by piece the armor is removed. She stood naked, exposed in all of her pain. I am flooded by the memories of my life that have caused such wounds. I understood how she had developed in response to that pain...how she had coped with the stress and the loss, and the price she had paid to keep me safe.

She was a part of me I wished I could ignore. I felt shame and remorse for wanting to turn away from her, for being repulsed by her scars.

But this was not a time for repulsion to dictate my actions.

"...I reach to offer my comfort and love.

She turns away in shame, then slowly responds and finally collapses in despair into my arms.

She tells me how hard she had tried to keep me safe, to protect my heart from the pain. When she lost Max she thought we would never be able to trust again. She was so angry at Spirit for taking him away. She

*makes it clear that she has no intention of cooperating
and going to D.C. She will never do anything God or my
Higher Self asks her to do again.*

*And she is enraged with me for taking the unneces-
sary risk with my new friend. He was sure to abuse the
friendship as well..."*

I felt compassion for her pain, but explained that
her version was not the entire story. We didn't have an
agreement with Sprit about Max. I understood her
pain, but her displacement of it had to stop. It was
about to gravely affect my career.

She acknowledged she did not want to do damage,
but defended her position based on my need.

"Her" argument carried a great deal of weight and
demanded that I now ask myself if I were ready to give
up such a protection. Was I ready to defend myself
without this armor? To trust again and rely on the
coping skills I had fathered along the way? Had I
healed enough to survive if I did not have her to carry
my wounds and to fight the battles for which I may be
ill prepared? Only time would tell if it were indeed safe.

Fortunately, the obstacles to my work did clear. I
was ambivalent, but felt it was time to get back on the
road. Two weeks later I was bound for Washington, D.C.
The impact of the work with my armored child, however, traveled with me. It followed me across the
states and set the stage for past and present to collide.

-----CHAPTER FOURTEEN-----

"Which Lifetime Is This Anyway???"

The work in Washington D.C. had gone well. Much to my surprise my passion for accompanying others on their journey to the caverns of their Soul had not diminished. The experiences of the previous year had augmented my confidence and talent. It was evident in the richness of my work. Max's absence, however, was also evident. The contrast between the me who instructed others on the healing of their childhood pains and the me who stood alone in that empty hotel room at the end of the day was unnerving. The tension culminated on that last night in Washington when a simple bath turned into one of the most incredible multidimensional experiences of my life.

It was as though a dark fog had rolled over the bay of my heart—simultaneously soothing and suffocating the sense of loneliness that penetrated me to the depth of my bones. The threat of loneliness and despair seemed unusually pronounced and ever present in the shadows of the unfamiliar and unknown.

And the chill—no matter what I did, I could not get warm. Feeling irritated that I had been caught in a September freeze at a hotel that did not provide central heat until October, I ran the water to take a hot, relaxing bath. I stepped into that tub unaware of what was about to occur. The chill, the void of being on the road without Max, the loneliness and despair all co-mingled and became the foundation for past and present to collide. Once they did I inadvertently crossed a line of no return and my life suddenly seemed unaffected by the boundaries of time.

"...It is 4:00 in the morning. I am restless. I cannot sleep. I cannot get warm. I run a hot bath and sink deep into the fluid comforter of warmth.

Still, I am chilled to the bone.

Suddenly and involuntarily, my body begins to rock. It is as if it is remembering something of which I have no conscious awareness.

I begin to weep...then whimper...whimpering and rocking, rocking back and forth, back and forth, holding myself, attempting to comfort myself in the midst of this unidentified despair.

My eyes naturally close and a visual image emerges in my mind's eye.

I am still me, but I am a different me.

I am still in a tub of water, but it is in another time and in an unfamiliar place.

I hear myself speak. "I am sorry. I cannot do it this time. I know I promised, but I do not know how to cope with this despair. I do not know how to proceed. I cannot get away from this grief. I cannot fulfill my contract. Please let me come home. I just cannot bear this despair..."

Without a clue as to whom to address, I continue to ask for forgiveness—to be set free.

"...My arms float freely in the water. I feel the sensation of blood dripping from my wrists, wrists that had recently been slit. My body goes limp as the liquid light slowly steals my last breath and I sink deeply into the welcoming arms of death...."

Half expecting to see red fluid seeping into the water, I cautiously opened my eyes. But the water was clear. I was in a bathtub in Washington D.C. I was not suicidal. Blood was not flowing from cut veins.

I was caught between two dimensions of time. Suicide is not an option for me in this life. I am too metaphysically oriented to believe it would relieve me of my pain. But I was witnessing a scene from my soul's past when this was not the case, a scene in which the despair had so engulfed my personality of that time that she had indeed taken her own life.

In my mind's eye, the blood was real, as was the peace I experienced when I finally succumbed to death. Inspired to continue, I again close my eyes.

"...The spirit escapes from this withered, lifeless body. It hovers above, suspended in time, waiting for someone to come and escort it into the Light.

And so I go. I take flight into another dimension of time to rescue a wounded part of my past. However, this time it is a fragment of my Soul from a different life lived many decades before.

I introduce myself as her future self, and then I ask her name. She says they call her Antoinette and asks if I have come to help. I assure her that she is now safe and promise to do what I can do so she can be freed to go home..."

After a few moments of pause I opened my eyes in awe and wondered how on earth I had just communicated with an aspect of my Soul who existed in a different dimension of time and space.

I had read about multi-dimensionality, but until that night in D.C. I had never before experienced the phenomenon. That night I had witnessed and experienced, simultaneously, a time from my soul's history when the despair had been so engulfing that I ended up taking my own life, an act for which I had no logical explanation.

Had I lost touch with reality? I found few comforts in the psychological world to support what had just occurred. In fact, I knew the only psychological references I did have would deem me quite mad!

Still, I wondered how many others had experienced a similar, multi-dimensional crisis. I wondered who else had suffered or was suffering from a pain for which there was no logical context.

In my own need to resolve this dilemma I began to discover that even though the identification of my disillusion and despair culminated in my experience in that bathtub in Washington D.C., it did not start there. It soon became obvious that Soul decisions and Soul patterns resulting from the events in Antoinette's life that led to her untimely suicide had impacted even the most minute endeavors pursued in my current life.

Her despair, when co-mingled with my own, diminished my capacity to trust and to love; disabled me from setting limits and appropriate boundaries; permeated every fiber of my self worth and hindered me from excelling to my professional capabilities. The bleedthrough of Antoinette's despair impacted the relationships I attracted, the professional choices I made, and the abundance I manifested. It influenced my self-image, my body image, even my spiritual pursuit.

I had no idea how many lifetimes I had been haunted by Antoinette's betrayal and despair, but I did know that I had been haunted for much of this one. With the assistance of my internal and spiritual support system, I started to follow the threads of Antoinette's pain back to a childhood experience in this lifetime when I felt a similar despair. Once there, I began to discover the common themes that wove her life to mine. Like a skilled shaman, I traveled—back and forth—between dimensions of time and began an endeavor that charted the course for my next pursuit—a journey into the unknown—a journey that would last another three years.

-----EPILOGUE-----

"Standing in the Light"

My inner work continued but it took me in a new, more multidimensional vein. The gift of the return of my heart however, came shortly after my first encounter with Antoinette. It started one fall day when I spoke at a Whole Life Exposition in San Francisco. After my talk, I looked around at the many booths. There was one that caught my eye. It was the booth of an Indian man who designed and drew medicine shields based on the date of one's birth. I decided to have mine done. He added that, for no extra cost, he could ask Great Mystery my given Indian name.

Several months later I came home after a weekend trip to find the piece of art in the mail. I open up this personalized, colorful Medicine Wheel. I was struck by several things. In the medicine wheel I am surrounded by the energy of Eagle, Deer, Otter, Sturgeon and Elk. Cupping my neck is the image of Raven. In the description it states that the Raven would bring illumination to my plights. It would be this energy that would assist me in shape-shifting my reality and in traveling to new sights. I remembered the many healings that White Raven had orchestrated for Max. Then my eyes were drawn to the top of the drawing and there it was in print.

In an instant I stepped into my future self and my name is "STANDS IN LIGHT."

That next spring it was again an anniversary of my father's death. I made arrangements to go home and spend the weekend with Mom.

I went to the cemetery and sat on the sacred ground that held the remains of Dad and Max. I reflected on the events of the last several years. I felt amazed at the healings that had taken place. I recalled the day that Max and I had said our good-byes. I marveled at how much of a teacher and a healer Max had truly been.

I was filled with love and gratitude for the two beings who had contributed so much to my growth. And I felt blessed to have the friends who had escorted me through this maze.

I closed my eyes to pay my respects and the following ceremony took place in my inner realm.

"...I am beckoned by the Angels.

We ascend and travel to this palace-like structure in the sky.

There are women, many beautiful women, draped in satin, Greek-like robes, walking around. They greet me and then carry on about their own business.

I am escorted to this sacred chamber.

Max and my new friend, Arthur, are waiting for me.

I walk up to them.

Arthur kisses me on the cheek and Max runs up to lick my hand.

Chief appears.

He holds a box in his hand. It is a beautiful, glass box...a box with no lid.

Chief beckons me to look. I do not touch. I just peek. I am taken back by its contents. Wrapped, very protectively, in a white satin cloth is my healed heart. It is radiant and is vibrating at a beat that resonates with the frequency of Mother Earth.

I am overwhelmed with tears, but they are gentle tears, tears that express hope and appreciation.

Arthur comes to my side and puts his arm around my shoulder. Max is at my feet.

Chief hands me the box. I cup the box in the palms of my hands.

I am not sure what to do.

In an instant my attire changes; I find myself clothed in a white satin gown. The cloth matches that which holds my heart.

With heart in hand, Arthur and Max lead me down a corridor to this open room. There is an aisle...at the end of this aisle there is a fern-lined arch. In the middle of the arch, there is a gleaming bright light. The aisle is flanked on both sides with rows of loved ones who have come to partake in the celebration.

Dad is waiting for me at the foot of the arch. He extends his hand. I turn to Arthur. We embrace. I bend down to bid Max good-bye, then Dad escorts me

*into the center of the arch. We embrace. I step for-
ward and stand, for the first time, in the center of the
light.*

*As I do so, my heart is transplanted back into my
chest. I feel an ache inside...and then energy shoots
through my entire physical form...every cell in my body
is being illuminated and recharged.*

*I am being reconnected to my God-Self. I am cere-
moniously being reunited with what had been so
severely shattered. My trust in my Highest Self is
once again restored.*

*My heart is pulsating to such a degree that I almost
feel nauseous. It is as if the very core of my being is
receiving a massage. There is this tremendous sensation of being complete...and a sense of expansion that
ripples out into the universe. Suspended in time, I
stand erect as I receive the healing of my heart.*

*The healing comes to a close and there is a gentle
tap on my shoulder. Feeling no need to be startled, I
slowly open my eyes and turn towards the gesture. I
see this light figure extending its hand. We walk
deeper into the light—out of the sight of all that have
come for the celebration..."*

The image next to me became clear. It was
Archangel Michael. He held up his sword as he asked
me to look deep into the red ruby of revelation.

As I did this I began to swirl back in time, back to
my beginning, before the experience of fear and sepa-
ration before abuse, abandonment and rage. I felt the

balance, the wholeness, the incredible sensation of complete and unadulterated love.

I was then told to breathe deeply, and I realized that my guidance was again expanding my heart, increasing its vibration, raising its frequency so I would be able to hold the truths that had been revealed.

"...I stand in a total state of receptivity until Archangel Michael motions for me to look again, into his glistening, ruby red stone. I begin to swirl—swirl through time and space, time and space, time and space. I keep swirling for what seems to be an eternity, and then the swirling stops. Archangel Michael stands before me with a book in his hand. It is the book that contains the history and "herstory" of my soul.

Every lifetime and every encounter I have ever had is recorded in my book.

Archangel Michael places the book in my hands then takes his place by my side. I ask him to direct me to the chapter that is relevant for me today.

I AM instructed to turn to Chapter 24. The title is "BALANCE." Balance and refinement—that is what I am to focus on this lifetime.

I AM to balance holding the connection I have in my heart and refine that connection so that whatever is sprinkled on my path I can shovel away much like I would scoop freshly dropped snow on a winter's day.

I AM not to judge or begrudge or feel victimized by that which appears before me. I am to seize the *opportunity to refine and to clean and to continually return to that state of grace that can exist, most purely, in the heart of my connection to my God-self.*

I AM to accept and embrace that the goal is to remain mindful of using all connections with others as a mirror to myself—knowing that there are to be no attachments to the form these connections will take.

I AM to stand back and watch, like the director of a play, what my Soul has written for my characters today.

I AM to observe the trials and the triumphs as they move through and challenge, in all dimensions of time and consciousness, all that stands between me and their connection to my maker.

I AM reminded of the previous instructions to share it when the time is right.

I AM told that by doing this I stand in the shoes of my new self and earn the right to Stand in the Light, to take my place as a teacher, healer and guide.

I close the book. The healing of my heart is complete.

Archangel Michael then motions for me to follow him. He escorts me down the aisle of Light back to the celebration. Arthur and Max await..."

I pause. I take a deep breath. I know there is more work to be done. I know Antoinette waits in another place and time. But as my eyes slowly open I decide to claim this precious moment as one of celebration. I look at Dad's headstone, at the picture of Max that sits by its side. I feel their presence. They are both right there, with me, ready to play. I look around the deserted area. No one is near enough to see. I grab my Indian drum. Dad, Max and I dance on their grave to its beat!

About the Author

Cathryn is licensed as an Addictions Counselor and Marriage and Family Therapist. She offers *Personal Life Coaching* to those who are interested in attaining holistic health. Please visit her website www.conscious-aerobic-exercise.com to hear about her most recent programs and adventures. She is available for individual consultations and can be reached at 612.282.3686 or via email ctinnerchildwork@aol.com

978-0-595-36279-0
0-595-36279-6

Printed in the United States
105954LV00002B/4/A